ENERGY
AND MOVEMENT

Britannica Illustrated Science Library

Encyclopædia Britannica, Inc.
Chicago ▪ London ▪ New Delhi ▪ Paris ▪ Seoul ▪ Sydney ▪ Taipei ▪ Tokyo

Britannica Illustrated Science Library

© **2009 Editorial Sol 90**
All rights reserved.

Idea and Concept of This Work: Editorial Sol 90

Project Management: Fabián Cassan

Photo Credits: Corbis

Illustrators: Sebastián D'Aiello, Nicolás Diez, Gonzalo J. Diez

Composition and Pre-press Services: Editorial Sol 90

Translation Services and Index: Publication Services, Inc.

International Standard Book Number (set):
    978-1-59339-845-3
International Standard Book Number (volume):
    978-1-59339-855-2
Britannica Illustrated Science Library:
    Energy and Movement 2009

Printed in China

ENCYCLOPÆDIA
Britannica®

www.britannica.com

Energy and Movement

Contents

The Elements and Matter

Page 6

Manifestations of Energy

Page 28

Energy Resources

Page 40

Uses and Applications

Page 66

The Engine That Runs Our World

At a moment in history that has been forgotten forever, but undoubtedly near the origin of humankind, people started to ask themselves how the world works and what it is made of. The first answers came in the form of supernatural explanations. However, with the advancement of knowledge, people discovered that there are physical laws that govern nature and that the knowledge of these laws is, in fact, attainable by human minds.

This book is a compilation of all the discoveries that were triggered by those two early basic questions. These discoveries, in turn, are the sum

FLOW OF ENERGY
Energy is a physical reality that exists everywhere in different forms. Energy, along with matter, constitutes the basis of all phenomena that take place in the universe.

of thousands of years of hard research, with all of its validations and errors. It is the story of misunderstandings that endured for centuries and of revolutionary ideas that brought acclaim, and sometimes even death, to those scientists who postulated them.

We shall begin by discovering what things are made of. In our imaginary laboratory, we shall analyze the properties of different substances and of the elements. With the help of an imaginary microscope, we shall investigate the atom, the smallest unit of matter that has the characteristic properties of a chemical element, as well as all of the fundamental particles that make up an atom-particles that were only discovered by science in the past few decades. We shall also classify elements and molecules according to their main characteristics and analyze all of the substances that impact our daily lives, such as plastics and metals.

We have dedicated a special chapter to new and amazing materials, such as aerogels, carbon fibers, and nanotubes. In the following pages, guided by the genius of Isaac Newton, we will discover how and why things move as well as the forces that are required to put things in motion. We shall also begin to explore one of nature's greatest mysteries: the force of gravity.

Subsequently, we shall learn some tricks to multiply force and, in this way, facilitate certain types of work that would otherwise be burdensome, or even outright impossible, for a single human being to perform. However, neither force nor movement are possible without energy. Therefore, later in the book, we shall dedicate several pages to studying energy. We shall discover that we can classify energy according to its characteristics, and we shall answer in a very simple and didactic manner a series of questions that are easy to pose but which require very complex answers, such as "What is light?," "What is heat?," and "What is fire?" We shall very carefully study phenomena such as sound, electricity, and magnetism. Using Albert Einstein's amazing theories of relativity, we shall learn that the conventional laws of physics behave differently when great forces or masses come into play, as they do at cosmic scales. We shall also learn that space and time are not equal or constant for everything or everyone and that they can vary according to the circumstances. We will find something similar when we study nature at a molecular or atomic level. This will prepare us for the world of quantum mechanics, an extraordinary place that, much in the same way as Alice when she ventured across the looking glass into Wonderland, will present us with apparently implausible phenomena, such as particles that can cross barriers as if they were ghosts going through a solid wall and particles that seem to occupy two different places at the same time.

We conclude this wonderful journey of science and imagination with an essential review of all types of energy sources available to humans. We shall study the advantages and disadvantages of each one of these energy sources (green, polluting, renewable, and nonrenewable), including sources yet to come that may open the door to a cleaner future for our species. This wonderful trip can begin as soon as you like; just turn the page.

The Elements and Matter

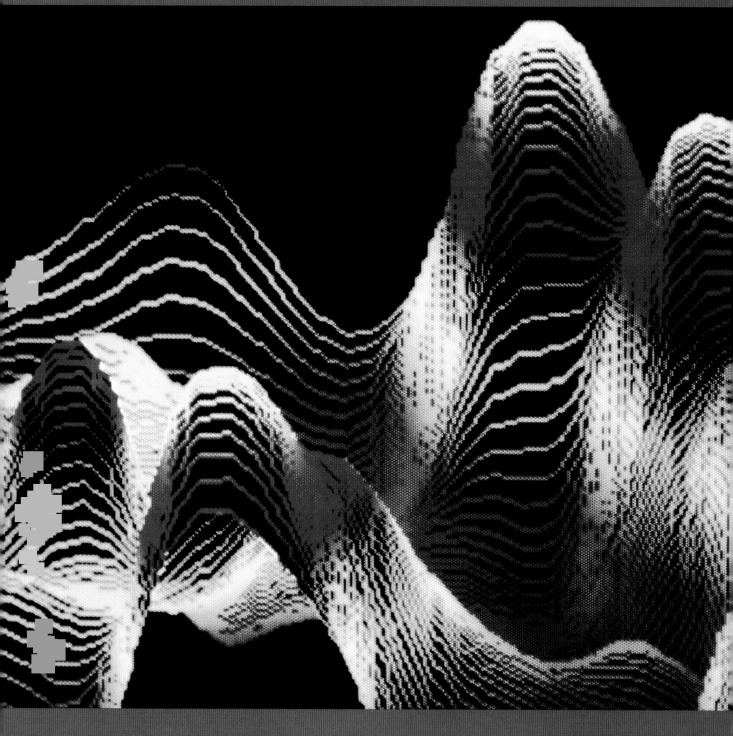

Almost 2,500 years ago, Democritus had a brilliant idea: it occurred to him that all things were made up of small indivisible particles, which he called atoms. Around the same time, other Greek philosophers decided that all things were the result of the combination of four basic elements: earth, air, water, and fire. Today we

NANOSCIENCE
The Scanning Tunneling Microscope (STM) is capable of penetrating the world of all that is minuscule. The wavelength of visible light has a thickness of 380 nanometers; that is to say, it does not pertain to the world of molecules.

MATTER 8-9

PROPERTIES OF MATTER 10-11

THE ATOM 12-13

THE ELEMENTS 14-15

CHEMICAL REACTIONS 16-17

METALS 18-19

POLYMERS 20-21

ACIDS AND BASES 22-23

RADIOACTIVITY 24-25

NEW MATERIALS 26-27

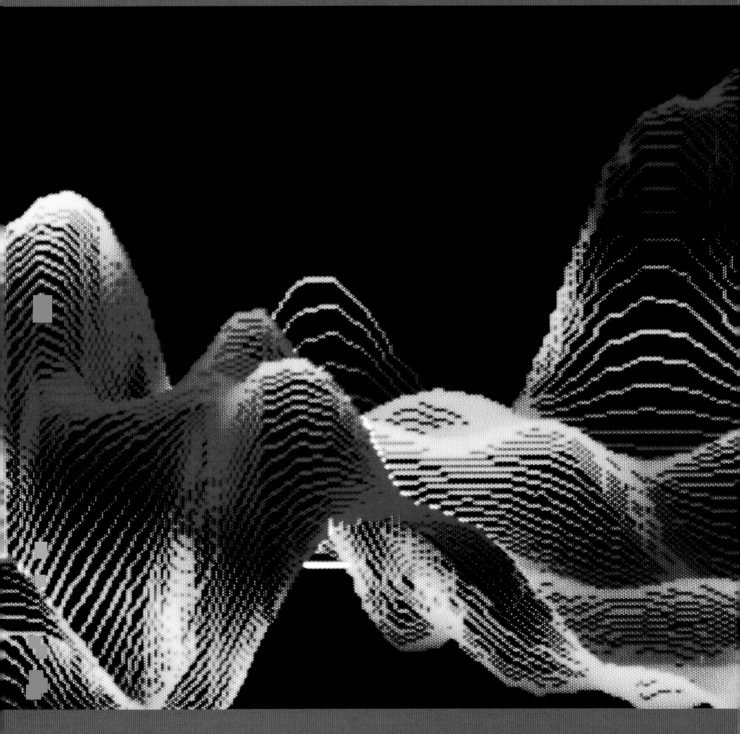

know that atoms can be divided and that the matter that surrounds us is a combination of 92 natural elements. We also continue to gain a deeper understanding of the structure of matter and the way in which atoms combine. This in turn has allowed us to create new materials: for example, lighter and stronger structures and cables that conduct electricity better. ●

Matter

Anything that takes up space and has a certain mass is considered to be matter. According to this definition, matter is something perceptible to human senses, without leaving out that which cannot be seen or touched, such as air or subatomic particles. It includes any physical entity in the universe that can be measured. In point of fact, however, the distinction between matter and energy is more complex, as matter can have wavelike (energy) properties, and energy can have particle-like properties. In addition, it has been known since Albert Einstein that matter and energy are interchangeable, as given by his famous equation $E = mc^2$. ●

Development

In the classical definition—which considers anything that has mass to be matter—matter is composed of atoms, something that people began to suspect more than 2,000 years ago, at the time of the ancient Greeks.

Atom

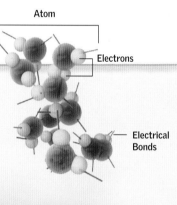

Electrons

Electrical Bonds

DEMOCRITUS

A Greek philosopher born in the middle of the 5th century BC, Democritus is considered the father of the atomist school. He postulated that reality is composed of two elements: what is (i.e., that which is composed of indivisible atoms) and what is not (i.e., that which is composed of the void in which those atoms move). He imagined that atoms differ in size, shape, and position and in their ability to combine or separate, forming other bodies. He thought that the human soul was composed of light atoms, and the body, of other, heavier ones.

Three States of Aggregation

Matter appears in three fundamental states of aggregation: solid, liquid, and gas. Changes in state depend fundamentally on temperature and pressure.

THE LIMITS

Above. . .

°32º F (0º C)

7,000º F (4,000º C)

9,000º F (5,000º C)

11,000º F (6,000º C)

12,500º F (7,000º C)

14,500º F (8,000º C)

16,000º F (9,000º C)

18,000º F (10,000º C)

20,000º F (11,000º C)

21,500º F (12,000º C)

. . .8,000º F (4,500º C), there are no solids.

. . .11,000º F (6,000º C), there are no liquids (only gases).

. . .18,000º F (10,000º C) matter exists only in the form of plasma.

Sublimation

Inverse Sublimation

-459.67º F (-273.15º C)

is the temperature known as "absolute zero," at which, according to classical physics, particles would cease all motion. Absolute zero is a theoretical limit that can be approached but never quite reached.

3 **SOLID STATE**

Particles acquire a crystalline structure. Solid bodies cannot be compressed, and they have their own shape.

① GASEOUS STATE

Particles do not form a crystalline structure.

There are almost no cohesive forces among the molecules, which move freely.

A gaseous substance fills all the space available in a container.

DARK MATTER

This is one of the greatest mysteries of science. Researchers have inferred from the gravitational behavior of the universe that much more matter must exist than that which is detectable by available means. They even believe that most universal matter exists in this form.

ANTIMATTER

This substance was first suggested in science fiction, but in recent decades its existence was not only proven but actually created in the laboratory. It starts from the premise that for every particle of the universe there is an identical counterpart, although with an opposite charge. If a particle and its antiparticle come into contact, they annihilate each other and generate a burst of energy.

Sublimation

A substance can change from a solid to a gaseous state without passing through a liquid state, a process known as sublimation. An example of this can be seen in "dry ice" (carbon dioxide ice).

Special States

There are at least two other unusual states in which matter may appear.

PLASMA

This involves a gas at high temperatures in which the atoms have broken apart and the electrons have separated from the nuclei. This characteristic gives plasma some special properties, such as the ability to conduct electricity. Plasma exists in the solar atmosphere or inside a fluorescent tube.

BOSE-EINSTEIN CONDENSATE

It is generated at temperatures near absolute zero (-459.67° F [-273.15° C]) and was achieved in a laboratory for the first time in 1995. Matter takes on special properties according to its composition, such as superconductivity, superfluidity, or a great ability to slow down the speed of light.

Evaporation

Condensation

② LIQUID STATE

Particles do not form a crystalline structure and move about freely.

The combinations among them are more powerful than in a liquid state.

The resulting body has fluidity and takes the shape of the container that holds it.

90%

of the universe could be made up of dark matter, according to various hypotheses; that is to say, the observable matter in the universe might be no more than 10 percent of the total.

Melting

Freezing

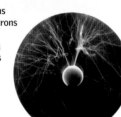

Properties of Matter

Different types of matter possess different properties that make them useful for certain applications. Titanium, for example, is strong and light at the same time; copper is a good conductor of electricity and can be drawn into wires to make cables. Plastic is not corroded by acids and can be used as a container. The examples are as innumerable as the properties and characteristics of substances. ●

Extensive Properties

These involve characteristics related to the quantity of matter, which make it possible to classify material bodies and systems, but which are not useful in themselves to identify the type of matter or material.

VOLUME

This refers to the space that matter occupies. In the case of liquids, volume is commonly measured in gallons or liters. Cubic feet or meters are customarily used for solids.

MASS

It is customarily defined as the quantity of matter present in an object, although for physicists, the concept is somewhat more complex. In classical physics, it is a constant measure and is measured in pounds or kilograms.

WEIGHT

The force of gravity is also a factor in defining weight, because weight involves the force that gravity exerts upon an object. The larger the mass, the greater the weight will be. Likewise, the greater the force of gravity, the greater the weight will be.

ANDERS CELSIUS

was a Swedish physicist and astronomer who lived only 43 years, from 1701 to 1744. Despite his contribution to the study of the aurora borealis and Earth's polar flattening, his best-known work was a temperature scale using the boiling and freezing points of water as its points of reference. He assigned the value of 0 to the first and 100 to the second, with 100 divisions in between. Later, his fellow Swede, Carl von Linné (also called Carolus Linnaeus), inverted the scale, which today is known as the Celsius scale.

Different Weight, Equal Mass

An average astronaut wearing a space suit weighs about 375 pounds (170 kg) on Earth.

Once on the Moon, where gravity is barely a sixth of that of Earth, the astronaut's weight will be less than 65 pounds (30 kg), making it possible to take great leaps.

The astronaut's mass, on the other hand, remains constant. It is the same on Earth and on the Moon.

1.4 billion

is, in tons, what 1/16th of a cubic inch (1 cm³) of a neutron star, the densest object known in the universe, would weigh on Earth. One-sixteenth of a cubic inch is equivalent in size to half a lump of sugar.

The same substance, but in different states of aggregation, may have different densities. This is the case for ice and liquid water. Despite the fact that exactly the same substance is involved, the density of ice is slightly less than that of water, and that is why it floats.

Intensive Properties

These do not depend only on the quantity of matter but also on the type of material. In many cases, they are functions of two extensive properties. The following are only a few examples.

4 DENSITY

arises from the relationship of the mass of a body to its volume. By definition, the density of water is taken to be 62.4 pounds per cubic foot (1,000 kg/m³).

Substance	Density (62.4 lb/ft³)	(1,000 kg/m³)
Water	62.4	(1,000)
Oil	574	(920)
Planet Earth	344.3	(5,515)
Air	0.8	(13)
Steel	490.1	(7,850)

When water and oil are mixed together, the water fills the lower part of the container because it is denser than oil.

OIL

WATER

5 SOLUBILITY

is the ability that some substances have to dissolve in others. They can be solids, liquids, or gases, and the degree of solubility depends on the temperature.

Effervescent tablets contain salts that dissolve in water and, as a product of the reaction, free a gas (in general, carbon dioxide). The gas, which is insoluble in this medium, escapes in the form of bubbles.

6 HARDNESS

is defined as the resistance a substance presents to being scratched by another. The substance with the greater hardness value scratches the one with the lesser hardness value.

Mohs Scale

is used in mineralogy and establishes the hardness of a mineral according to a table.

Mineral	Hardness
Talc	Passing a fingernail over it is sufficient to scratch it.
Gypsum	A fingernail can scratch it, but with greater difficulty.
Calcite	It can be scratched with a coin.
Fluorite	A knife can cause a scratch.
Apatite	A knife pressed with some force will scratch it.
Orthoclase	Steel sandpaper scratches it.
Quartz	It scratches glass.
Topaz	It scratches quartz.
Corundum	It scratches topaz.
Diamond	It is the hardest natural mineral.

7 MELTING POINT

It is commonly defined as the temperature at which a solid becomes a liquid. However, the correct definition of melting point is the temperature at which the same substance coexists in a liquid and a solid state.

8 BOILING POINT

It is generally defined as the temperature at which a liquid substance becomes gaseous. However, it is more accurate to say that it is the maximum temperature that a liquid can reach. This parameter depends on the type of substance, as well as on pressure.

9 CONDUCTIVITY

is the ability of a substance to allow an electric current, heat, or sound to pass through it. Metals tend to be good electrical conductors. Copper is a good example. It is often used in power cables.

10 OTHER PROPERTIES

In addition to the ones mentioned above, there are numerous other intensive properties for classifying materials. These properties include refractive index, tensile strength, viscosity, and malleability.

The Atom

For a long time, the atom was thought to be the elementary and indivisible particle of the universe, but it has now lost this label. Today it is well known that atoms are made up of smaller particles, which, in turn, can be subdivided into even smaller, more primordial particles. The atom, however, continues to be considered the smallest part of a chemical element that preserves the properties of that element. For example, a gold atom is the smallest particle that maintains the properties of gold. If an atom is divided, the resulting protons, electrons, and neutrons will not differ in any way from those that make up the atoms of other elements.

A System in Miniature

Atoms are composed of three types of particles—protons, neutrons, and electrons—which differ from one another, in particular, by the type of electric charge they have. The first two (protons and neutrons) form the atomic nucleus. Electrons, on the other hand, orbit the nucleus at very high speeds.

Electrons
orbit the nucleus, and their charge is negative. They are much smaller than protons and neutrons. An electrically neutral atom has as many orbiting electrons as protons in its nucleus.

Atomic Number
The number of protons (+) defines the atomic number. For example, nitrogen has an atomic number of seven for its seven protons.

JOSEPH JOHN THOMSON
This British physicist (1856-1940) discovered the electron in 1897. This discovery had enormous implications for science because it confirmed the suspicion that the atom was not an indivisible entity, as had been believed for many years. Although Thomson even succeeded in calculating the mass of the electron, he could not generate a convincing model of atomic structure, a task which his colleagues completed years later. He was awarded the Nobel Prize for Physics in 1906 for his experiments on the movement of electricity through gases.

Nucleus
This is made up of protons (with a positive charge) and neutrons (with a neutral charge). There are typically about the same number of protons as neutrons, although this is not always the case.

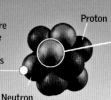

Proton

Neutron

First Shell
It accepts up to two electrons.

Second Shell
It accepts up to eight electrons.

1

is the number of protons and of electrons that hydrogen has. It is the lightest and most abundant element in nature.

Energy Levels
Electrons are grouped in shells located at different distances from the nucleus. Two electrons in the same shell orbit at the same distance from the nucleus, even if the orbits are different.

Although in this diagram the orbits are similar, in reality they can be more or less eccentric.

1,840

electrons collectively have the same mass as a single proton.

The forces that keep the electrons orbiting the nucleus are some of the strongest found in nature.

QUANTUM NUMBERS

No two electrons in the same atom have the same orbit. For that reason, using four parameters known as quantum numbers, it is possible to individually identify them, inasmuch as there are no two electrons with the same four numbers.

Number	Use
Principal Quantum Number (n)	Indicates the distance of the orbit from the nucleus.
Azimuthal Number (l)	Indicates the eccentricity of the orbit.
Magnetic Number (m)	Indicates the spatial orientation of the orbit.
Spin (s)	Indicates the direction of the orientation of the electron's spin.

Almost all the space occupied by an atom is the space taken up by the orbits of its electrons. The vast majority of an atom's mass is concentrated in its nucleus. If an atom were the size of a golf ball, the electron would orbit the golf ball at a distance similar to the height of the Eiffel Tower: 1,000 feet (324 m).

Protons and Neutrons from the Inside

For a long time, it was thought that protons and neutrons were elementary and indivisible particles. Today it is known that each one is made up of three quarks, bound together by gluons. Electrons, on the other hand, are elementary and indivisible particles.

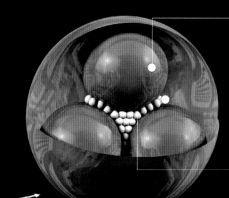

Quarks

are bound together by very strong forces and are never found "free" in nature. They can be separated for a fraction of a second during high-energy particle collisions that are generated in particle accelerators.

Gluons

These are particles without mass or electric charge that interact with quarks and are partially responsible for their remaining bound together.

Isotopes

In some cases, although two atoms of the same element have the same number of protons, they may have a different number of neutrons. In that case, they are isotopes. Isotopes tend to have very different properties from one another.

ISOTOPES OF OXYGEN

The main isotope of oxygen has eight protons and eight neutrons in its nucleus, in addition to eight orbiting electrons. Oxygen has two other known stable isotopes and 14 unstable isotopes.

8 protons
8 neutrons

One isotope, Oxygen 18, has eight protons and 10 neutrons, in addition to eight orbiting electrons.

8 protons
10 neutrons

The radioactive isotope Oxygen 12 has eight protons and only four neutrons, in addition to eight orbiting electrons.

8 protons
4 neutrons

Probability Calculations

Based on more complex scientific developments, such as quantum mechanics and the uncertainty principle, among others, it is considered impossible to determine the exact position of an electron at a given moment. For this reason, the representation of an atom with its electrons is actually approximated by a probability formula, which gives the likelihood of finding the electrons in any particular locations at any given moment.

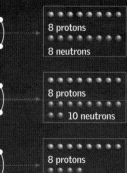

90% of Total Probability

Probability calculation for the hydrogen atom, which has a single electron

The Elements

The chemical elements are those substances that are impossible to divide into simpler substances. Alone or in combination, they make up all the visible matter of the universe. There are 118 known elements, but only 92 of them are found in nature. The rest are products of the laboratory. Although in essence elements seem very similar to one another, because they are all formed from atoms, and therefore from electrons, protons, and neutrons, their properties can vary radically. For better identification and classification, they are organized into a periodic table.

DIMITRY MENDELEYEV

To this Russian scientist, born in Siberia in 1834, we owe the solution to a problem that preoccupied chemists for a long time: the correct classification of the elements. Mendeleyev achieved this using a periodic table, which he published in 1869. The table also made it possible, many years later, to discover chemical elements that had never been seen before but were predicted in the table. Mendeleyev died in 1907.

The Periodic Table

Developed in the middle of the 19th century, it permits the classification of the elements on the basis of two parameters: the number of energy levels or orbits into which their electrons are grouped and the number of electrons in their outermost energy level, or valence shell.

Periods

The electrons orbit the atomic nuclei grouped in different energy levels. The period indicates how many levels of energy an atom has. Even so, atoms within the same period usually have different properties.

Alkaline Metals

are very chemically reactive elements, which is why they are usually found in compounds and almost never in a pure state. They are soft metals with a low density. The most abundant is sodium.

Alkaline Earth Metals

are also soft, very reactive, low-density metals, although they are somewhat less reactive than the alkaline metals. They react with water to form extremely alkaline solutions. The most abundant of this group are calcium and magnesium.

Transition Metals

are hard, with high boiling and melting points, and are good conductors of electricity and heat. They can form alloys with one another. Iron, gold, and silver are some examples.

Lanthanoids (or lanthanides)

are relatively abundant elements on Earth and are usually found in the form of oxides.

Groups

indicate how many electrons an atom has in its valence shell. The atoms of one group usually share properties and similar characteristics.

SYMBOLS

Symbol and Number of the Element

Atomic number: Indicates the number of protons in the nucleus of an atom.

Mass number: Indicates the mass of the atom as compared to an atom of carbon (with a value of 12).

Radioactive element.

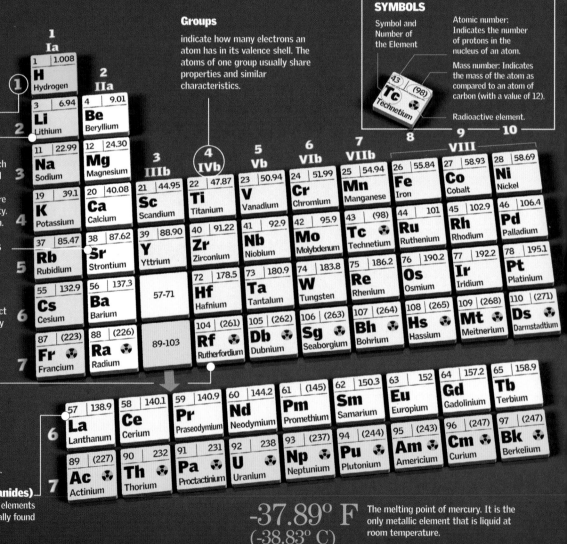

-37.89° F
(-38.83° C)

The melting point of mercury. It is the only metallic element that is liquid at room temperature.

Types of Elements

Beginning with their structural characteristics, atoms can share certain characteristics and thus be grouped into different types.

Metalloids

have properties intermediate between the metals and the nonmetals. One of the most important is that they are semiconductors (their electric conductivity is between that of metals and that of insulators). They are very important in the manufacture of transistors and rectifiers and are components of integrated circuits. Among the most significant are silicon and germanium.

Other Metals

are soft with a low melting and boiling point. Some outstanding examples are aluminum, tin, and lead.

Nonmetals

are some of the most abundant elements on Earth. They include hydrogen, carbon, oxygen, and nitrogen, which are present also in living beings. They are very electronegative and are poor conductors of heat and electricity.

Halogens

are highly electronegative elements. They have important industrial applications.

Noble Gases

With eight electrons in their last energy level, they are extremely stable and not prone to reacting with other elements. They include neon, argon, and xenon.

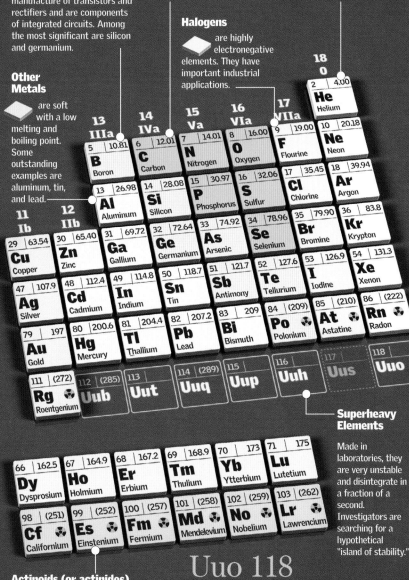

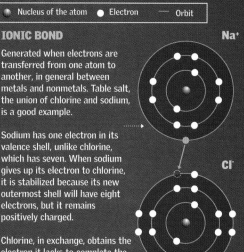

Superheavy Elements

Made in laboratories, they are very unstable and disintegrate in a fraction of a second. Investigators are searching for a hypothetical "island of stability."

Actinoids (or actinides)

Most of these elements are not found in nature (they were synthesized in laboratories), and their isotopes are radioactive.

Uuo 118

Ununoctium is the last element in the periodic table; it was first created in the laboratory in 2006. It is highly unstable. Although only three nuclei were produced in the 2006 experiment, it is thought that the element could be a gas at room temperature, with properties similar to those of the noble gases.

Bonds

For an atom to be stable, it must comply with the "octet rule." That is to say, it must have eight electrons in its valence shell, as is the case with the noble gases, which are not very reactive with other atoms. When the number of valence electrons differs from eight, atoms try to obtain, give up, or share electrons with other atoms, in order for each to have eight valence electrons. In the process, they form bonds and, therefore, create molecules with new properties.

• Nucleus of the atom   • Electron   — Orbit

IONIC BOND

Generated when electrons are transferred from one atom to another, in general between metals and nonmetals. Table salt, the union of chlorine and sodium, is a good example.

Sodium has one electron in its valence shell, unlike chlorine, which has seven. When sodium gives up its electron to chlorine, it is stabilized because its new outermost shell will have eight electrons, but it remains positively charged.

Chlorine, in exchange, obtains the electron it lacks to complete the eight in its valence shell and is negatively charged. The union is sealed.

COVALENT BOND

The atoms join together but do not lose or gain electrons: they share them. This is the case for carbon dioxide (CO_2), water (H_2O), and methane (CH_4).

Carbon dioxide (a gas we exhale) consists of one atom of carbon with four electrons in its valence shell and two of oxygen, which each have six valence electrons. Thus, each atom of carbon shares two of its valence electrons with each atom of oxygen, and all three therefore obtain the eight atoms for their outermost energy level.

METALLIC BONDS

These occur between the metallic elements. Here, the electrons are not gained, lost, or shared; rather, they float freely in a kind of sea of electrons. This characteristic is what permits metals to be good conductors of electricity. Electric current is nothing other than a current of electrons.

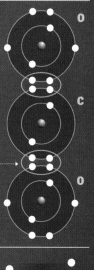

Chemical Reactions

C hain reactions occur constantly in nature, during industrial processes, within the human body, and in almost any other environment imaginable. When two or more substances come into contact, under certain conditions the atomic and molecular links break and generate new molecules, thus creating different substances with new properties. In a given reaction the reagents may be completely consumed, but the quantities of matter remain unchanged, even while new compounds are being formed and even under different states of aggregation. 1

A whole chemistry lab inside a simple match

The simple act of lighting a match unleashes a complex chemical reaction by which different molecules combine with oxygen in a process that releases heat and which the human eye perceives as fire.

Lighting It Up

The match head contains potassium chlorate ($KClO_3$) (a compound that is often present in explosives) and stibnite (Sb_2S_3). The head is struck against a special surface usually made up of a ground crystal and red phosphorus (sandpaper) base.

1 The friction created by the head of the match against the striking surface turns some of the surface's red phosphorus into white phosphorus. The white phosphorus, which is very flammable, catches fire as soon as it is exposed to the air.

2 The heat given off by the white phosphorus found in the striking surface unleashes a chemical reaction in the match head in which the oxidizing agent ($KClO_3$) produces oxygen. Oxygen and heat generate the ignition of the Sb_2S_3. This fire then begins to consume the base of the match, which is made of combustible material.

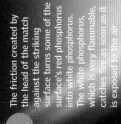

ANTOINE-LAURENT LAVOISIER

Lavoisier was born in Paris in 1743 and is considered one of the fathers of chemistry. Among the valuable contributions he made to this branch of science was his description of the important role that oxygen plays during the process of combustion and fire. He also postulated the law of conservation of mass. Lavoisier died in 1794.

Heat

is one of the fundamental conditions for producing or accelerating a chemical reaction. Cold, on the contrary, slows down this process.

Types of Reactions

Chemical reactions may be classified according to the characteristics that are inherent to the processes they create. The following are some of the most common ways to group them.

Reversible and Irreversible

A reaction is irreversible when it only takes place in one direction and the original reagents cannot be recovered. In reversible reactions it is possible to recover the original reagents under certain conditions.

The decomposing processes of organic compounds, for example, are a product of irreversible reactions.

Oxidation and Reduction

A metal or a nonmetal loses electrons and, therefore, oxidizes. In the reduction reaction, the metal or the nonmetal gains electrons. When in contact with oxygen, the iron oxidizes and generates a red-colored compound: iron oxide.

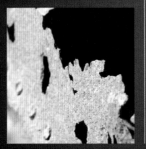

Combustion

A combustible substance, generally organic, combines with oxygen, releasing heat, water, carbon dioxide, and carbon monoxide. Engines that run on hydrocarbons, such as gasoline and diesel, operate because of a combustion reaction.

Exothermal and Endothermal Reactions

During exothermal reactions, heat is released. During endothermal reactions, heat is absorbed. The transformation of a raw egg into a hard-boiled egg implies a series of endothermal reactions that occur only if heat is present. Fireworks, on the other hand, release heat, which is a product of exothermal reactions.

Law of Conservation of Matter

One of the main laws of natural science, it states that, after a chemical reaction, the mass of the reagents is the same as the mass of the products. This is because there is no loss of matter in this process; rather, matter undergoes a transformation.

Reagents

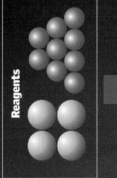

Chemical Reaction

Products

Catalysts

are substances that can accelerate or delay chemical reactions and that are not consumed during the reaction. Catalysts are very important elements in nature and in industrial processes.

The Language of Reactions

Chemical equations enable us to represent reactions with signs and symbols.

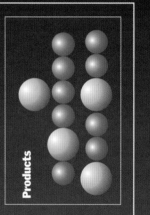

Quantity of atoms or molecules

"Reacts with . . ."

"Produce"

Products

Reagents

$$2Mg + O \Leftrightarrow 2MgO$$

It means that two magnesium atoms react with one of oxygen, making two molecules of magnesium oxide (MgO).

Metals

What we usually refer to as metals are certain pure chemical elements, such as iron or gold, as well as certain alloys, such as bronze and steel. Metals were first used almost 7,000 years ago, and since then, they have become an essential part of life for human beings. They are present in monumental constructions such as bridges and buildings, in mass transport vehicles such as boats and planes, in guns, and in all other types of accessories. Another characteristic of metals is their capacity to conduct electricity, which makes them prime players in the world of engines, energy, and communication. ●

Purification

In general, metals are usually found in nature in combination with other elements (forming different kinds of minerals). Their use, therefore, requires special purification processes, as in the case of iron.

1 The ingredients are placed in the furnace. They start to burn and melt at high temperatures.

THE INGREDIENTS

Iron Ore
contains iron in the form of oxides. Atoms of iron are oxidized—that is, combined with oxygen. They must be separated in the process so that the iron reaches the pure metallic state.

Coke
is the furnace's fuel. However, it also produces carbon monoxide as it burns, which reacts with the oxygen atoms of the iron oxide and removes them. Pure metallic iron is produced in this way.

Lime
During the process, lime combines with silicates present in the iron ore. This prevents the silicates from combining with and contaminating the iron once the oxygen is removed.

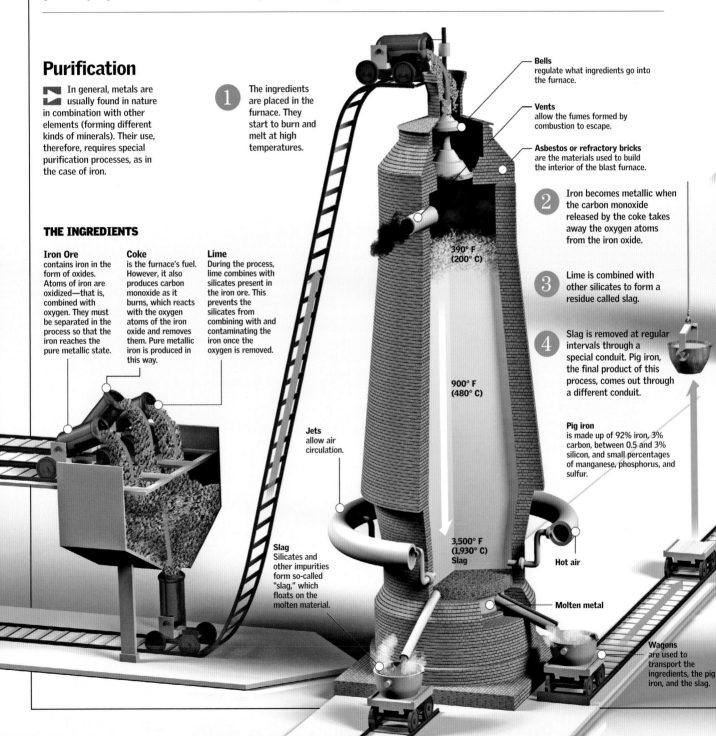

Bells
regulate what ingredients go into the furnace.

Vents
allow the fumes formed by combustion to escape.

Asbestos or refractory bricks
are the materials used to build the interior of the blast furnace.

2 Iron becomes metallic when the carbon monoxide released by the coke takes away the oxygen atoms from the iron oxide.

3 Lime is combined with other silicates to form a residue called slag.

4 Slag is removed at regular intervals through a special conduit. Pig iron, the final product of this process, comes out through a different conduit.

Pig iron
is made up of 92% iron, 3% carbon, between 0.5 and 3% silicon, and small percentages of manganese, phosphorus, and sulfur.

Jets
allow air circulation.

Slag
Silicates and other impurities form so-called "slag," which floats on the molten material.

390° F
(200° C)

900° F
(480° C)

3,500° F
(1,930° C)
Slag

Hot air

Molten metal

Wagons
are used to transport the ingredients, the pig iron, and the slag.

Alloys

Metals can form alloys with other elements to form substances with new properties. This is the case with steel, one of the most important raw materials in the world.

STEEL PRODUCTION

Carbon mixes with the atoms of iron in the pig iron but does not combine with them chemically, as in the case of oxides. Through metallurgical processes, the quantity of carbon is reduced. To obtain this reduction, it is forced to combine with oxygen. Steels with over 3 percent carbon are hard but brittle.

IMPROVING WHAT IS GOOD

In addition to iron and carbon, steel alloys typically contain aggregates of other elements that give them their special attributes.

+Molybdenum
It increases steel's hardness and makes it stronger.

+Chromium
It makes steel "stainless." Kitchen utensils or appliances are examples.

+Zinc
It is used to coat iron and create galvanized steel. It is resistant to corrosion.

HENRY BESSEMER

A British engineer born in 1813, Bessemer developed a process that greatly improved the performance of steel production. Because of his innovations, he is considered the father of the modern steel industry. His method allowed him to reduce the proportion of carbon present in iron and to obtain a stronger product at a much lower cost. This greatly stimulated the development of steel production at the end of the 19th and early 20th centuries. Bessemer died in 1898.

GOLD

Unlike iron, gold is a far less reactive metal, and it is frequently found in nature in a pure state.

5 Pig iron is poured into the smelting furnace.

6 Oxygen is injected; it reacts with carbon and forms carbon monoxide. By doing this, the proportion of carbon present in pig iron is reduced.

7 The use of lime helps remove impurities such as phosphorus.

Generally, the carbon content of steel is not more than 2 percent, and it is usually between 0.2 and 0.3 percent.

8 The steel obtained can be converted into bars for storage, which can be treated later.

3,450° F (1,900° C)

The temperature that the interior of the blast furnace can reach.

Properties

The unique attributes of metals have made them irreplaceable in people's daily lives.

CONDUCTIVITY

In metals, the external electrons are weakly bound to their nuclei. For this reason, the nuclei in metals seem to float in a sea of electrons. This phenomenon is what gives metals their property of electric conductivity. Electric conductivity is, precisely, a flow of electrons. Metals are also heat conductors.

SOLIDS

In general, metals at room temperature are solid, with varying degrees of resistance and hardness.

MALLEABILITY

Despite their solid state, metals can change their shape. In some cases, it is even possible to shape them as fine as threads. This, combined with their electric conductivity properties, makes them the ideal material for making wires or cables.

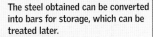

Polymers

The discovery of polymers and chemists' ability to synthesize them in laboratories, and even to create new ones, led to the formation of new materials. Some of these materials, such as plastics and synthetic rubber, had such impressive attributes that they quickly became an important part of people's daily lives. In addition, biologists and biochemists discovered that polymers are essential for the inner workings and structure of living things.

LEO BAEKELAND
The father of plastics was a Belgian chemist born in 1863. While working in the United States, where he owned a factory for producing one of his own inventions (Velox photographic paper), he accidentally discovered a synthetic resin that he named Bakelite. This invention not only won him worldwide recognition but also marked the beginning of the "era of plastics." Baekeland died in 1944.

Infinite Chains

Polymers are vast chains made up of hundreds of thousands of smaller molecules known as monomers, which are linked together by a process of polymerization. Wool, silk, and cotton are all natural polymers. Other polymers such as nylon and plastic are the product of laboratory processes.

POLYMERIZATION
During polymerization, in this case of Bakelite (the first synthetic plastic), monomers unite and yield a polymer and water.

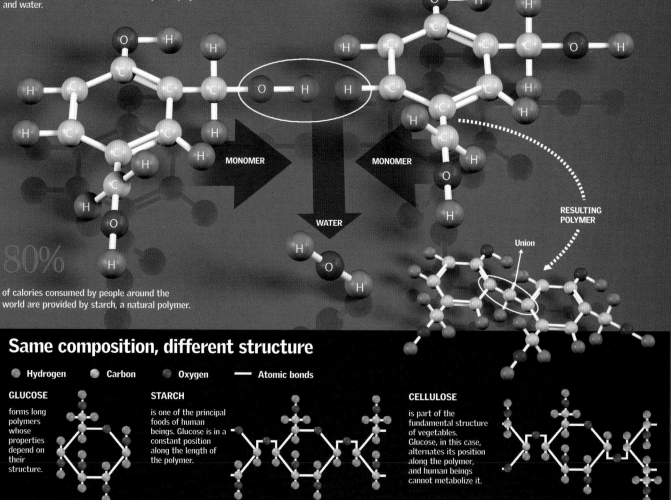

MONOMER

MONOMER

WATER

RESULTING POLYMER

Union

80%
of calories consumed by people around the world are provided by starch, a natural polymer.

Same composition, different structure

- ● Hydrogen
- ● Carbon
- ● Oxygen
- — Atomic bonds

GLUCOSE
forms long polymers whose properties depend on their structure.

STARCH
is one of the principal foods of human beings. Glucose is in a constant position along the length of the polymer.

CELLULOSE
is part of the fundamental structure of vegetables. Glucose, in this case, alternates its position along the polymer, and human beings cannot metabolize it.

Plastics

When plastics, a special kind of polymer, first made their appearance, they revolutionized industry, methods of production, and the chemistry of common objects during the 20th century. They are inexpensive, moldable, and colorful. They are good electric insulators, can be rigid or flexible, and are very durable.

APPLICATIONS

for plastics appear to be countless. There are many types of plastics that are useful for different needs.

Most plastics produced in the world are used for containers and packaging, followed by plastics specifically made for the construction industry, and then by plastics engineered for use in electric equipment.

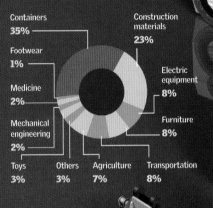

Containers
35%

Footwear
1%

Medicine
2%

Mechanical engineering
2%

Toys
3%

Others
3%

Agriculture
7%

Construction materials
23%

Electric equipment
8%

Furniture
8%

Transportation
8%

RECYCLING

The durability of plastics, one of their most outstanding qualities, also creates a problem because degradation of plastics takes centuries and causes environmental contamination. For this reason, the recycling of plastics is important.

60 million

tons, constitute the annual world production of polyethylene (the simplest polymer).

Noble Gases

comprise six very stable, almost inert elements that tend not to react with other elements. For this reason, in nature they are not found combined with other elements. They are gases at room temperature.

The naturally occurring noble gases are helium, neon, argon, krypton, xenon, and radon. The last one is radioactive.

PROPERTIES

Because it is very stable and less dense than air, helium is ideal for filling up blimps. Some of the noble gases, such as neon, glow when they move through an electric current, for which reason they have often been used for colorful lighting displays. They are also used as a coolant in refrigeration systems.

EXCEPTIONS TO THE RULE

Xenon is capable of reacting with fluorine, which is the most electronegative of all elements, and some compounds have even been created with krypton.

Nonmetals

comprise 12 elements, many of which are of great importance and abundance in nature. Oxygen and carbon are good examples. They are very electronegative and are therefore prone to generating compounds.

PROPERTIES

Nonmetals are very bad conductors of heat and electricity. Some of them are gases, such as oxygen and chlorine, and others are solids of varying hardness and little luster, such as iodine and phosphorus. In their purest form, they usually appear as diatomic molecules: for example, O_2, F_2, Cl_2, and so forth.

ABUNDANCE

Nonmetals are not only the most abundant elements in the outer layers of the Earth, but they also are the main ingredient in all living things.

Diamond

Acids and Bases

Why does lemon taste sour? Why is the sting of a bee so painful, and why does putting some vinegar on it provide relief? Why is it dangerous to touch the liquid in car batteries? All these questions can be answered by looking at the properties of some of the substances that, when in contact with water, become acids or bases. This classification is actually centered on the behavior of such substances at a microscopic level: substances with a propensity of giving hydrogen ions (protons) are acids, and those capable of accepting protons, and therefore removing them from their environment, are bases. •

Under the Microscope

▲ In an aqueous environment, acids and bases increase their concentration of protons (H+) or of oxide ions (OH-), respectively, which gives the substances special properties.

NEUTRAL WATER

Water molecules consist of two hydrogen atoms and one oxygen atom (H_2O). The quantity of protons (H+) is similar to that of hydroxide ions (OH).

ACID

When an acid is added, for example with hydrochloric acid (HCl), the molecule separates into ions (H+ and Cl-). Thus, the concentration of protons (H+) surpasses the concentration of hydroxide ions (OH-), and the substance becomes an acid.

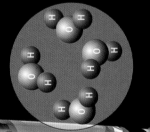

Properties

Acids and bases have properties that make them very useful for different applications.

ACIDS

- Have a sour taste
- Are good conductors of electricity (hence their use in batteries)
- Release hydrogen gas when in contact with metals
- Are corrosive

BASES

- Have a bitter taste
- Are good conductors of electricity in aqueous solutions
- Neutralize the action of acids, forming water and salt
- Are corrosive

Corrosiveness is one of the most interesting characteristics of acids. Even though they can affect organic substances and metals, they do not react with plastics.

Strong and Weak

When acids are dissolved in water, one should not only take into account the concentration (the amount of acid present in the entire substance) but also whether the acid is strong or weak.

If the union between the hydrogen protons (H+) and the rest of the molecule that forms the acid is strong, then the dissociation of the acid in the water is of little importance. Only a few protons will be free. The others will continue to be tied to their molecules. This is a case of a weak acid.

When the union between protons (H+) and the rest of the acid's molecule is weak, the dissociation can be complete, generating a great quantity of free protons. These are strong acids, which, in the right concentration, can be corrosive. Sulfuric acid is a good example.

Buffer

In many living things, such as humans, changes in the level of pH can be lethal. This is why the body produces buffer solutions that neutralize the changes in pH when new agents, such as food, vaccines, and so forth, enter the body.

SOREN P.L. SORENSEN

This Danish chemist, born in 1868, is known for developing, in 1909, the concept of potential of hydrogen (pH) to measure the acidity of solutions and for describing some of the methods to determine pH. Sorensen was also a pioneer in the study of acid amines. He died in 1939.

BASE

A base such as sodium hydroxide (NaOH) dissociates when dissolved in water into Na+ and OH ions. This means that it provides hydroxide ions to the solution. In this way, the quantity of oxide ions will surpass the quantity of protons (H+), turning the substance into a base, or alkali.

Measuring Acidity

The acidity of a substance is measured in terms of pH, which is determined through different methods.

Substance	pH	
Gastric juice	1.5	The lower the pH level, the greater the acidity.
Lemon juice	2.4	
Cola beverages	2.5	
Vinegar	2.9	
Coffee	5.0	
Milk	6.5	
Pure water	7.0	7.0 is the neutral pH level. If the level is higher than 7, then the substance is alkaline.
Hand soap	10.0	
Ammonia	11.5	
Bleach	12.5	

Radioactivity

One of the most surprising discoveries of the late 19th century was that some chemical elements release high-energy radiation capable of interacting with matter. In time, scientists discovered that what caused this phenomenon was the fact that unequal energy balances between protons and neutrons in the nucleus of radioactive isotopes made them unstable. In adopting more stable structures, these isotopes released different kinds of radiation and turned into other chemical elements. Today nuclear energy produced by this phenomenon has important applications in medicine, the generation of electric power, and production of the most lethal weapons known. ●

ERNEST RUTHERFORD
The father of nuclear physics was born in New Zealand in 1871. Among his many contributions and discoveries were his work describing alpha and beta radiation and his work determining the kind of radiation that is related to the disintegration of elements. This latter work was something scientists at the time considered an impossibility. Rutherford, who also discovered the atomic nucleus and studied its characteristics, was awarded the Nobel Price in Chemistry in 1908. He died in 1937.

A Powerful and Invisible Force

As they become more stable, radioactive isotopes experience changes in which they release various forms of energy.

ISOTOPES

Stable
In stable atoms, the number of positively charged protons and neutrally charged neutrons is the same or almost the same.

Protons

Neutrons

Radioactive
The number of protons is different from the number of neutrons. The atom is thus unstable. In its attempt to stabilize, it undergoes changes and, consequently, releases energy in different forms.

Protons

Neutrons

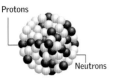

RADIATION
When a radioactive isotope modifies its energy level seeking a more stable configuration, it releases three kinds of radiation.

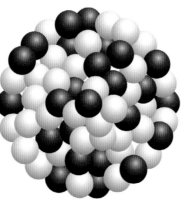

Gamma Radiation (γ)
This is the most harmful and energetic form of radiation. Gamma radiation consists of electromagnetic waves, which are released when the nucleus of an isotope slips to a lower level of energy and becomes more stable.

Alpha Radiation (α)
The atom releases two protons and two neutrons—that is, a helium atom's nucleus. Therefore, its atomic number (Z) decreases by two units, and its mass by four. Uranium-238 (Z 92), for example, becomes thorium-234 (Z 90).

Beta Radiation (ß)
The atom releases an electron and a positron (its equivalent, but of opposite charge). This way, the atomic number changes by one unit, and the mass by two units.

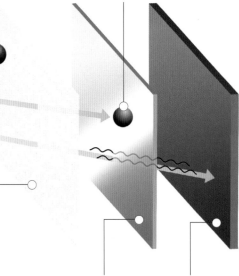

α particles travel at 1/10 of the speed of light and cannot go through a piece of paper.

ß particles travel at half the speed of light and can penetrate a piece of paper but cannot penetrate an aluminum sheet.

γ rays travel at the speed of light, and because of their great energy, they can only be stopped by materials with high atomic numbers, such as lead or thick armor.

From One Element to Another One

As the radioactive isotope decays and releases radiation, its structure and energy levels are modified until it reaches stability. In the process, it transforms into other isotopes, forming so-called "decay chains."

URANIUM-234 DECAY

Isotope	Uranium-234	Thorium-230	Radium-226	Radon-222	Polonium-218	Lead-214	Bismuth-214	Polonium-214	Lead-210	Bismuth-210	Polonium-210	Lead-206
Emission	→α	→α	→α	→α	→α	→α	→α	→α	→ß	→ß	→α	→ stable
Half-life	245,000 years	8,000 years	1,600 years	3,823 days	3.05 minutes	26.8 minutes	19.7 minutes	0.000163 second	22.3 years	5.01 days	138.4 days	

Half-life

A radioactive isotope may decay in a matter of seconds or of millions of years. Given a quantity of a radioactive isotope, the half-life is the time it will take for one-half the quantity to decay.

Uranium-235, used in atomic weapons, has a half-life of 700 million years.

Cobalt-60, which is used in radiotherapy, has a half-life of 5.3 years.

The half-life for oxygen-15, a rare radioactive isotope of oxygen, is 122.2 seconds.

40

is the approximate number of radioactive isotopes present in nature. The rest, more than a thousand, were created by humans.

Fission and Fusion

Atomic nuclei may, under certain conditions, split apart or fuse together. Both processes release enormous quantities of energy, which has led to their use in electric-power generation and in nuclear weapons.

FISSION

Once triggered, fission can be used to produce a chain reaction.

1 A "fissile" nucleus is bombarded with neutrons.

2 As it accepts the neutron, the nucleus becomes so unstable that it fragments into two smaller nuclei. As it does so, it releases ß radiation, free neutrons, and a large amount of energy.

3 The free neutrons, expelled at high energy, induce the fission of new nuclei, generating a chain reaction.

Neutron

Neutron

Neutron

Nucleus of the atom of Uranium-235

Energy

Chain reactions are used to heat water and produce electricity from the steam released in nuclear reactors.

150,000

was the number of casualties caused by the atomic bomb dropped by the United States on the Japanese city of Hiroshima in 1945.

FUSION

Under conditions of high pressure and temperature, two atomic nuclei (which naturally tend to repel each other) fuse, forming a new and heavier element. In the process they release large quantities of energy.

Unlike fission, fusion is, for the time being, not profitable for energy production, because inducing it in a controlled manner has required as much or more energy as what is generated.
Nuclear fusion occurs naturally inside stars. It is the mechanism that keeps them "shining."

Formation of the Helium-4 nucleus

Hydrogen-2 nucleus

Hydrogen-3 nucleus

Expulsion of one neutron

New Materials

The creation or discovery of new materials has often led to drastic changes in world history and in the daily lives of individuals. This happened with bronze, iron, steel, petroleum, and plastics, to mention just a few. Today, thanks to advancements in physics, chemistry, and computer science, the field of new materials has become highly promising. In recent years, it has been stimulated by the development of nanotechnology, which works at the atomic and molecular levels and could unleash a true revolution in the future. ●

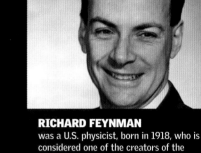

RICHARD FEYNMAN
was a U.S. physicist, born in 1918, who is considered one of the creators of the concept of nanotechnology. During his youth, he participated in the development of the atomic bomb. He then dedicated most of his career to research in quantum mechanics, for which he received the 1965 Nobel Prize for Physics. In 1959 he held a conference titled "There's Plenty of Room at the Bottom," which many consider to be the beginning of nanotechnology. He died in 1988.

The Marvels of Carbon

▶ Carbon, which, depending on its structure, can assume the form of graphite or a diamond, can also be transformed into materials with unique qualities that are, little by little, starting to replace conventional materials on a large scale.

Fibers

Extremely fine carbon fibers embedded in a supporting polymer produce a light, strong material. This microscope image shows a carbon fiber, with a diameter of a hundredth of a millimeter, compared to a human hair.

Different Structures
Fibers can be organized into different structures, giving the material distinctive properties.

Radial

Random

Concentric rings

Linear

Radial waves

Trilinear

PROPERTIES

• High strength with an outstanding flexibility ratio

• Low density: much stronger and lighter than a variety of metals

• Very good thermal insulator

• Resistance to several corrosive agents

• Fire-retardant properties

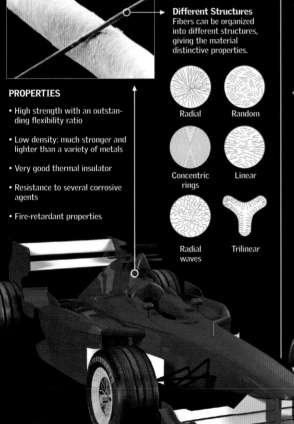

Nanotubes, Microscopic Marvels

One of nanotechnology's rising stars is the nanotube, which has atomic-level dimensions. It is made of sheets of carbon wrapped into a tube that measures only a few nanometers in diameter—that is to say, a billionth of a meter.
Nanotubes are among the strongest materials known. They are 100 times stronger than steel. They are also excellent conductors of electricity, hundreds of times more efficient than copper.

SIZE
0.6 to 1.8 nanometers in diameter

PROPERTIES

• They are one of the strongest structures known even though their density is six times less than that of steel.

• They can carry enormous quantities of electricity without melting.

• They have great elasticity. They recover their shape after being bent in sharp angles.

10,000
is the ratio of the diameter of a carbon fiber to that of a nanotube. Nanotubes, moreover, can measure up to a millimeter in length, which makes them the longest known structure, in relation to their diameter.

The Mysterious "Frozen Smoke"

Aerogel is one of the newest and most promising materials, despite its cloudlike appearance. Some of the main characteristics of aerogel are its strength despite its light weight (almost as light as air!) and its amazing thermal insulation capacity.

INSULATING PROPERTY
The aerogel is a powerful thermal insulator, which makes it extremely attractive for many applications.

COMPOSITION
There are aerogels made of silica, carbon, and other materials, even though the biggest proportion of the compound (up to 98%) is always air.

GREEN INSECTICIDE
Some types of aerogels are ground into such a fine powder that they can block the respiratory tracts of insects.

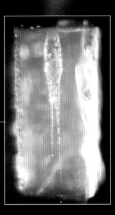

Air
98%

Solid
2%

FILTERS AND CATALYSTS
Because of their cavernous structure, they are excellent filters and great catalysts. NASA used them to collect particles from the comet Wild-2.

STRENGTH
It is surprisingly high considering how light the material is.

DENSITY
Aerogel is 1,000 times less dense than glass and only 3 times heavier than air.

The mouth of the blowtorch can reach 2,400° F (1,300° C).

Metamaterials

Are materials that, when treated and reorganized at nanometric scales, acquire properties that do not exist in nature. They are at an early developmental stage, and their first applications are associated with the field of optics.

The Dream of Invisibility

One of the most surprising properties of metamaterials is the development of materials with a negative index of refraction. This opened the way to a new invention that, up to that point, had seemed closer to science fiction than to reality: a "cloaking device," or an invisibility shield. Scientists from Duke University achieved this feat in an experiment in 2006, although they used microwaves instead of natural light.

Wave

Object

Invisibility layer

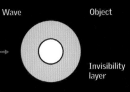

1 An electromagnetic wave approaches an object covered by a metamaterial "layer of invisibility."

2 The wave enters the layer and is bent around the object.

3 The wave recovers its form without distortion. The layer does not produce any reflection, so the object is "invisible."

Manifestations of Energy

W e live in a world in motion, even when we barely take a moment to think about it. But, why is it that when we throw something into the air, it lands on the ground? What is it that keeps our feet on the Earth? A creative search for answers to these and many other questions led Isaac Newton to formulate a series of laws that

TURBINE
Picture of a machine that
transforms the flow or pressure
of a fluid into rotary motion.

FORCE 30-31   MOTION 36-37

GRAVITY 32-33   SIMPLE MACHINES 38-39

PRESSURE 34-35

eventually evolved into the starting point of classical physics. For there to be motion, there must be forces that, when combined, generate a series of surprising effects, such as the possibility that a sailboat pushed by the wind can travel in the direction opposite this very wind. Forces can be multiplied with the aid of machines. This allows us to work with less effort.●

Force

A lthough the word *force* usually brings to mind a powerful locomotive or a weight lifter in the midst of a competition, to physicists this concept must be defined in terms of any interaction capable of moving an object at rest or changing the velocity or direction of an object already in motion. Understanding the concept of force and determining its nature and how it functions were great unsolved mysteries until the end of the 17th century, when Isaac Newton wrote what is considered the first modern definition of this phenomenon. Today scientists are attempting to understand the so-called basic forces of nature at a deeper level. ●

Anatomy of a Push

A basic example of force acting on an object: the cue stick strikes the white ball at rest, imparting a force that results in motion. The white ball does the same thing with the other balls after colliding with them.

Acceleration
As a result of the force acting on the white ball, it reaches a certain level of acceleration.

Static Force
There are forces that in certain situations act without producing motion. This ball, even at rest, is really subject to the force of gravity. Nevertheless, because it is resting on top of a solid base, it cannot move until being hit.

Linear Motion
results from the collision of an object in motion with another one at rest, and the force is defined as the acceleration of the object multiplied by its mass.

Contact
In the case of the game of pool, the forces are contact forces, because contact is necessary in order for there to be any interaction between the object and the force. Magnetism and gravity, on the other hand, can be defined as noncontact forces, or forces that act at a distance.

SIR ISAAC NEWTON

Considered by many as the greatest scientist of all time, Isaac Newton was born in England in 1642. His contributions to several fields of science are numerous and invaluable, such as the law of universal gravity and the laws that bear his name, which became the base of classical mechanics. Other fields to which Newton made fundamental contributions include mathematics—with the development of integral and differential calculus—and optics. He died in 1727.

Deceleration
If a new force is not applied, the balls will tend to slow down because of friction with the table.

Combining and Balancing Forces

Forces can be combined and balanced to generate different effects. When balancing, the strongest forces prevail, although they are perturbed by the action of others.

An arm-wrestling tournament is a good example of balancing forces: the wrestler that applies the most force with his arm is the winner.

Thanks to the combination of different forces, a sailboat can travel windward—that is, in the direction from which the wind is blowing.

Measuring Force

➤ A dynamometer is used to measure force, and the values are expressed in newtons in the International System of Units.

DYNAMOMETER
This device was invented by Isaac Newton. It works by means of a spring that stretches as more force is applied to one of its ends.

THE NEWTON
Unit used to measure force. A newton (N) is equivalent to the force that, when applied to a mass of 1 kilogram (kg), experiences an acceleration of 1 meter (m) per second per second (s^2).

FORMULA

Force   Kilogram   Meter

$$1N = \frac{1kg \times m}{S^2}$$

Second Square

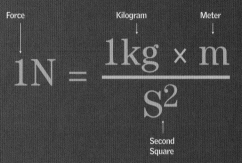

Contact or Noncontact

➤ One way of classifying the forces takes into account whether there must be physical contact to produce the interaction.

CONTACT FORCES
The objects must "touch" each other in order for the force to be effective.

NONCONTACT FORCES
The transmission of force is not through contact. This can be seen in gravitational attraction and magnetism.

100,000 newtons is the force a jet turbine is capable of generating.

Magnet ⸻

Force ⸻

Metallic Element ⸻

Fundamental Forces

➤ Physicists, concerned with describing the basic forces of nature, discovered four fundamental interactions with matter that cannot be broken down into other more simple ones. Currently, they are attempting to explain them as different expressions of one force.

Gravity
Responsible for the weight of objects and the motions of the stars. At an atomic scale, it exerts very little influence, and for that reason, it is not included in quantum theories. It is thought to be transmitted by the graviton, a particle that has not been detected.

Electromagnetic
This force links electrons to atomic nuclei. It gives structure to materials, and it is related to electromagnetic radiation. In modern models, it is unified with the weak nuclear force.

Weak Nuclear Force
A force that acts at the subatomic level, with particles such as quarks and leptons, and gains importance in radioactive-decay processes. Like gravity, it is a purely attractive force.

Strong Nuclear Force
Unlike the gravitational force, it acts at a very short distance. It keeps the protons and neutrons together in the atomic nucleus, overcoming the repulsion between particles of the same polarity, such as protons.

These fundamental forces govern all processes and motion in the universe.

Gravity

ravity is one of the most ubiquitous phenomena in the lives of people, as well as one of the most studied by scientists. Yet at the same time, it is also the least understood of nature's phenomena. Its effects have been known since the origins of humankind. People have always instinctively known that if things are dropped they fall. But scarcely four centuries have passed since Isaac Newton developed the mathematical equations that allow us to measure and quantify this effect. And scarcely a century has elapsed since Albert Einstein postulated a more complete approximation of the workings of the force of gravity in his General Theory of Relativity. Either way, gravity is the most elusive of all the forces when one tries to find explanations that link the fundamental forces of nature.

JOHANNES KEPLER

Kepler was a German astronomer and mathematician who is considered to be one of the greatest scientists of all time. Born in 1571, Kepler is remembered for his laws about the motion of the planets around the Sun. He discovered that the planets' orbits were not perfect circles, but rather ellipses, and his scientific work was fundamental in Isaac Newton's later theories about motion. He died in 1630.

Free Fall

Gravity is an attractive—never repulsive—force generated by any body with mass, even by small objects such as a cup of coffee or the human body.

Galileo Galilei demonstrated that two objects, even with different masses, experience the same acceleration in free fall.

In a vacuum, a feather would fall at the same speed as a piece of lead. But on Earth, the lead will fall first because the air generates greater resistance to the shape of the feather.

The feather and the lead also generate a gravitational force, but because of their small masses, this force is barely noticeable.

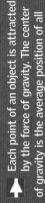

Attraction of Heavenly Bodies

The planets, the Moon, and the stars exert powerful gravitational forces that extend beyond their own bodies and affect their neighbors.

THE MOON AND THE SEA
The force of Earth's gravity keeps the Moon "trapped" on average some 239,000 miles (384,000 km) away.

Center of gravity

Each point of an object is attracted by the force of gravity. The center of gravity is the average position of all the points and, in effect, where the entire weight of the object is concentrated.

The tightrope walker is able to stay on the tightrope by moving his arms to each side to control his center of gravity.

6.96 miles/s (11.2 km/s)

is the speed any object requires to escape Earth's gravity . . . and never return.

The acceleration generated by the force of gravity on Earth is equal to 32 feet (9.8 m) per second squared. That is, for each second that goes by, the object accelerates by 32 feet (9.8 m) per second.

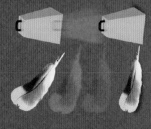

New moon First quarter Full moon Last quarter

A New Vision: Relativity

After some time, the equations based on the gravitational theories of Isaac Newton were discovered to be slightly off, especially when applied to gravitational forces of great intensity. Albert Einstein solved this problem by thinking of gravity in a different way in his General Theory of Relativity, published between 1915 and 1916.

For Einstein, gravity was not a force but rather the visible result of deformations of space-time because of the presence of masses.

CHAMPIONS OF GRAVITY

Black holes, the result of the presence of supermassive or hyperdense objects, generate a gravitational field so strong that no particle, not even light, can escape them. This is why it is impossible to "see" them, and they can only be detected by using indirect methods.

According to Einstein's novel vision, space curves around a mass. Therefore, a ray of light that brushes past this mass will be deflected because of the curvature of space. Einstein predicted this deflection precisely, and it was confirmed experimentally during an eclipse.

Sun

Ray of light

3-g

or 3 times the force of gravity, is what the human body typically experiences on a roller coaster ride.

The car in the roller coaster does not reach an acceleration of 32 feet (9.8 m) per second per second because it is slowed down by the friction forces caused by the rubbing of the wheels against the rails and of the cars against the air.

THE PLANETS

Because they possess different masses, the planets in the solar system have different gravitational strengths. On Mars a person's weight would be less than half what it is on Earth. On Jupiter, on the other hand, a person would weigh more than twice as much as on Earth. In a hypothetical stroll over the surface of the burning Sun, a person would weigh 27 times more than on Earth.

DISCOVERY OF NEPTUNE

Beginning in 1821, astronomers noted apparent perturbations in the orbit of Uranus and predicted the presence of a planet whose gravitational force would be responsible for such anomalies. Years later, they even calculated the planet's position. In 1846, the existence of the planet was confirmed through direct observation through a telescope. This is how the planet Neptune came to be discovered.

CELESTIAL BODY	g
Sun	27.90
Mercury	0.37
Venus	0.88
Earth	1.00
Moon	0.16
Mars	0.38
Jupiter	2.64
Saturn	1.15
Uranus	0.93
Neptune	1.22
Pluto	0.06

Pressure

Pressure is one of the plethora of phenomena that human beings had knowledge of, and took advantage of, even before they could explain them. When we fill up a balloon with air, or stare in amazement at a fakir lying on a bed of nails, when our ears hurt if we dive deep under water, or when we admire the power of a bulldozer, the underlying concept of pressure is present. Science defines pressure as the result of a force applied over a surface area. This concept applies to solids, liquids, and gases. In the case of gases, the effect of temperature is also important.

6,200 HP

is the amount of power that could be generated by the "big boy" locomotives of the Union Pacific railroad in its day, using just steam to move the wheels. This is equivalent to the power of almost four diesel locomotives.

The history of the railroad could not have been written were it not for steam and the steam engine.

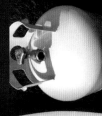

When a gas is compressed under great pressure, it becomes a liquid. This phenomenon has important practical applications, especially that of storing great quantities of a gas in smaller volumes than the same substance would take up if left in a gaseous state.

The Force of Gas

Although gases seem to be invisible or even undetectable masses, they can exert great pressure—so much pressure, in fact, that they are capable of moving a train or a turbine to generate electricity.

Inside the balloon, the gas generates the pressure that keeps it inflated.

Molecules, in their chaotic motion, collide repeatedly with the walls of the container (in this case, the balloon), thus generating the phenomenon of pressure.

BLAISE PASCAL

His contributions to the understanding of the concepts of pressure and vacuum garnered this French chemist, physicist, and religious philosopher, born in 1623, a special recognition: his name is used as the unit for measuring pressure. But Blaise Pascal was so versatile that his inventions included the hydraulic press, the syringe, and what was probably the first mechanical calculator. He dedicated the last days of his life to religion, philosophy, and theology. He died in 1662.

Pressure, from the top of the atmosphere to the depths of the sea

The atmosphere that surrounds planet Earth and the water that makes up the seas have weight and, therefore, generate pressure, which varies at different altitudes and depths.

ATMOSPHERIC PRESSURE

defined as the force exerted by the air over the surface of the planet. Because it is related to Earth's gravity, the pressure (weight) of the atmosphere increases as one gets closer to the surface. It is measured in pascals and, on average, equivalent to 101,325 pascals, which in other units is equal to 1,013.25 millibars, 1 kilogram per square centimeter, or 14.7 pounds per square inch.

THE EFFECT OF TEMPERATURE

Temperature plays an important role in the pressure of gases.

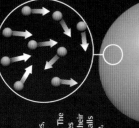

As the temperature drops, the molecules move at slower speeds and collide with the walls of the balloon less frequently.

At higher temperatures, the motion of the molecules accelerates. The energy of the molecules and the frequency of their impacts against the walls of the balloon increase, and the pressure is therefore greater.

At an altitude of more than 60 miles (100 km) above the Earth's surface, in space, atmospheric pressure ceases to exist. At this altitude, astronauts must use pressurized suits to survive.

At 66,000 feet (20,000 m) above sea level, water boils at room temperature. The environment is uninhabitable.

At an altitude of 33,000 feet (10,000 m) above sea level, cabins in commercial airplanes must be pressurized because of the low pressure and lack of oxygen.

At 26,000 feet (8,000 m), on the tallest mountain peaks, it is necessary to use a respirator or oxygen mask because the air is very thin and the pressure is very low.

Up to 15,000 feet (4,600 m) above sea level, it is possible to fly without the use of a pressurized cabin. At this altitude, there are also some inhabited cities, such as La Paz (Bolivia).

At sea level, the average pressure is 1,013 millibars.

A human can dive to a depth of 400 feet (120 m).

Because of their reinforced structures, submarines can dive to a depth of several hundred meters under the sea.

At a depth of 10,000 feet (3,000 m), there is a rich diversity of life, despite the cold, darkness, and high pressure. Sperm whales and giant squids can dive to this depth.

The greatest ocean pressures are found within the Marianas Trench, in the Pacific, at more than 33,000 feet (10,000 m) below sea level.

WATER PRESSURE

is the weight of water on the surface of Earth, and it increases with depth.

The Fakir's Secret

How does the fakir manage to lie down over a bed of sharp nails and not be pierced by them? The secret, besides his courage, is to trust the mechanisms that determine the behavior of pressure.

Pressure is defined as the effect of a force on a given surface area. This means that a given fixed force acts with greater intensity over a small surface than when the force is spread out over a larger area.

If the weight of the fakir (the force) were to rest over a single nail, the surface over which the force would act would be very small and the nail would pierce the fakir's body.

Because the fakir is lying over a large number of nails, the force is spread over a much larger surface, and the nails do not pierce his body.

Trieste

The name of the bathyscaphe that submerged in the Marianas Trench, the deepest point in the ocean, in 1960. At 7 miles (11,033 m) below sea level, a pressure of 1,086 bars (15,751 pounds per square inch) was measured.

20,000 m

10,000 m

10,000 m

Motion

From atoms to stars and planets, the entire universe is in a constant state of motion. However, it took thousands of years for humans to comprehend this phenomenon and postulate the first laws that explain it (which were born from the acute observations of Isaac Newton). An object needs a force to change its motion. ●

JOSEPH-LOUIS LAGRANGE

Born in Turin, Italy, in 1736, this mathematician, astronomer, and physicist is renowned for his countless contributions to science, among them the mean-value theorem, numerous works on algebra, and Lagrangian mechanics, with which he reformulated Isaac Newton's postulates. With the aforementioned mechanics, he was able to simplify Newton's formulas and calculations by starting from the idea that all solid and fluid mechanics arise from a single fundamental principle. Lagrange was also a prolific astronomer. He lived in France and Prussia and died in 1813.

In Action

An object in motion follows a trajectory, which depends on the type of forces that act over it and—on the surface the Earth—on resistance produced by phenomena such as friction.

ACCELERATION AND DECELERATION

When velocity varies, we call this "acceleration." If the variation has a constant value, then the motion is "uniformly accelerated," or "uniformly decelerated" if the variation is negative.

Friction

On the surface of the Earth, the dart experiences the resistance that is produced by its contact with the air (friction). Its horizontal velocity decreases from this resistance, as its vertical velocity increases from the Earth's gravitational attraction.

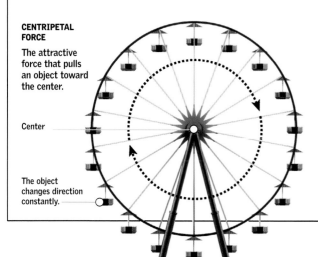

18.6 miles/second (30 km/s)

is the velocity at which the Earth travels through space relative to the Sun. Thanks to inertia, however, we hardly notice it.

HOW FAST CAN THEY MOVE?

Light	300,000 km/s
Voyager spacecraft	55,000 km/h
Fighter jet	3,500 km/h
Sound (in air)	1,125 km/h
Sports car	330 km/h
Cheetah	90 km/h
Human	36 km/h
Snail	0.05 km/h
Tectonic plates	3 mm/year

Circular Motion

is easily observed in car wheels, in fans, and in many amusement park rides, such as the Ferris wheel. The object is attached to the center of the circle, which forces it to constantly change direction.

CENTRIPETAL FORCE

The attractive force that pulls an object toward the center.

Center

The object changes direction constantly.

CENTRIFUGAL FORCE

An object in circular motion experiences a "centrifugal force" that, contrary to the centripetal force, gives the impression of propelling it outside the circle. In reality, it is not a force but inertia, which makes the object tend to move in a straight line.

Friction

When two bodies come in contact, frictional forces are generated between them that act as resistance to the motion. Thanks to these forces, shoes grip the floor, car brakes function, and we are able to grasp objects with our hands without their falling.

Thanks to the fact that friction turns the kinetic energy of bodies into heat, we can light a match.

To reduce the force of friction, special liquids are used, such as oils and greases (lubricants).

3,000° F (1,650° C)

is the temperature to which the space shuttle is subjected by friction with the air as it reenters the Earth's atmosphere at high speed.

INERTIA AND LINEAR MOTION

Objects cannot change their state of rest or motion by themselves. They require an outside force to do so. This property is termed "inertia." Therefore, in a vacuum away from any masses, the dart would conserve its motion indefinitely. Likewise, an object in motion has a certain "linear momentum," a parameter that depends on its mass multiplied by its velocity. The greater the mass and velocity, the greater the linear momentum will be.

Linear motion can also be transferred between objects. If the target were not affixed to a surface, the dart, upon giving up its linear momentum during the collision, would cause it to move.

SPEED

If we measure the time it takes the dart to travel a given distance, then its "speed" can be determined.

$$\text{Speed} = \frac{\text{Distance}}{\text{Time}}$$

Uniform straight-line motion

Gravity

Parabolic motion

The dart follows a parabolic path. On one hand, it tends to move in a straight line (straight linear motion), but on the other, it is attracted by the force of gravity (uniform accelerated motion) toward the Earth's surface. This combination results in a parabolic motion.

Newton's Laws

In the 17th century, Isaac Newton postulated the laws that explain motion, which became one of the greatest contributions to physics of all time.

1st LAW

States that an object remains at rest or in motion without changing state, unless an outside force acts on it.

2nd LAW

States that upon applying a force, an object changes its state (from rest to motion, a change in direction or in speed) and that the change is related to the strength of the force.

3rd LAW

States that for every action there is an equal and opposite reaction. In this case, the helicopter moves in the opposite direction to the thrust of the propeller.

Simple Machines

A re simple and ingenious, and they ease daily chores. They are plentiful in any mechanical device that has mechanical components, and they start with a basic premise: they must be capable of modifying forces by magnifying them, decreasing them, or changing their sense or direction. However, because of the law of conservation of energy, the energy input to a machine will be exactly equal to the output, although likely distributed differently. ●

Multiplying Forces

The simple act of riding a bicycle implies making use of a series of machines that allow us, by barely moving our feet, to travel at a speed much greater than we could reach by running.

GEARS

They are especially useful for magnifying or decreasing a force, as well as for changing its direction.

If a toothed gear is meshed with another one with more teeth, then the second one will turn more slowly, but with less effort. In a bicycle, this gear relationship is used to go up hills. The bicycle feels "lighter" but requires more pedaling not to loose speed.

If a toothed gear is meshed with another one with fewer teeth, then the second one will turn faster, but it will require more effort. Cyclists use this relationship to achieve greater speeds with less pedaling, although the bicycle feels "heavier."

INCLINED PLANE

It allows loads to be raised to a certain height while exerting less force. However, to reduce the effort, the angle of the inclined plane must be reduced; that is, the distance between the starting and ending points must be increased.

Mountain roads tend to make zigzags. The engine uses less force to take the vehicle to the top, although it must travel a greater distance. Therefore, the amount of energy needed is conserved.

SCREW

Uses a principle similar to the inclined plane and is based on ridges around a cylinder or cone. The greater the number of ridges, the smaller the effort needed, although a greater number of turns will be required to tighten the screw.

PULLEYS

are especially useful to lift loads vertically, through ropes and wheels that change the direction of the force.

The greater the number of wheels and ropes, the smaller the effort that must be applied to lift the load. However, the length of the ropes will be longer, so the amount of work is maintained.

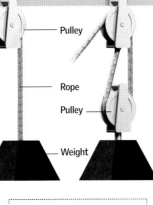

Pulley

Rope

Pulley

Weight

COMPLEX MACHINES

are machines that are made up of more than one simple machine. In the bicycle, for example, we can find gears, axles, wheels, and pulleys that optimize the bicycle's performance.

LEVER

One of the simplest machines, it consists of a bar that, when combined with a fulcrum, magnifies the force and allows the lifting of heavy loads with a relatively small effort, although this effort must be applied over a longer distance.

Types of Levers

1st Class

The fulcrum (pivot) lies between the force and the load. The longer the force arm is relative to the load arm, the greater is the gain in force.

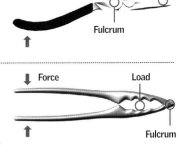

Force   Load

Fulcrum

2nd Class

The load is located between the force and the fulcrum. The longer the force arm is relative to the load arm, the greater is the gain in force.

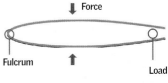

Force   Load

Fulcrum

3rd Class

The force is applied between the fulcrum and the load. Rather than gaining force, it loses it, but it allows for greater control of the load.

Force

Fulcrum

Load

223 tons

can be lifted by a K-10,000 crane, which, with its 400 feet (120 m) in height, is the largest in the world. It uses a complex system of pulleys divided into six sections.

ARCHIMEDES

The most notable scientist in antiquity, he was born about 287 BC in Syracuse, Sicily, when the city was a Greek colony. Among his many inventions and discoveries, most of which were fundamental to the later development of science, are the Archimedes' principle (pertaining to buoyancy) and the study of the lever. The lever had been known to the world for a long time, but Archimedes provided a theoretical framework to explain it. He is well known for his now famous statement about the lever: "Give me a fulcrum, and I shall move the world." He died in 212/211 BC during the siege of Syracuse by the Romans.

AXLES AND WHEELS

When force is applied to an axle, as in the case of bicycles, the speed is multiplied because the edge of the wheels spin faster.

With each turn of the axle, the wheel will travel a greater distance because it has a greater circumference.

If the force is applied to the edge of the wheel—the handlebars of a bicycle or the steering wheel of a car—then it becomes possible to multiply the force at the axle.

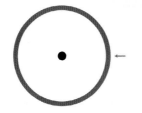

Energy Resources

FILAMENT
Picture (magnified by 200 times) of a filament that produces light by incandescence when an electric current passes through it.

The universe's energy is a unified force and is never lost. It can adopt different forms, be transformed, and even remain latent, manifesting itself under certain conditions, as in the case of an object suspended in air that is then suddenly dropped. Light, heat, and electricity are some of the forms in which energy is manifested. In this

ENERGY AND WORK 42-43
HEAT 44-45
MAGNETISM 46-47
ELECTRICITY 48-49

CIRCUITS 50-51
ELECTROMAGNETISM 52-53
SOUND 54-55
LIGHT 56-57

SPECIAL RELATIVITY 58-59
GENERAL RELATIVITY 60-61
QUANTUM MECHANICS 62-63
QUANTUM COMPUTER 64-65

chapter, you will learn about energy and also discover the new theories that revolutionized physics during the early years of the 20th century: relativity—which explains the functioning of the cosmos on a universal scale, where energy, mass, and velocities can acquire impressive magnitudes—and quantum mechanics, which describes how the world works on an atomic scale. ●

Energy and Work

The universe is energy. In the functioning of each subatomic particle and of each living being, in the occurrence of any terrestrial or atmospheric event, regardless of its scale, energy performs an essential role. However, it is not a thing—not something tangible. In general, when people speak of energy, they are really referring to its visible effects, such as light, heat, or motion. Energy, moreover, cannot be created or destroyed. It only changes form; it is transformed. To better understand it, it is possible to classify it according to the characteristics by which it manifests itself. ●

Mechanics of Motion

The concept of mechanical energy arises from the study of objects from the standpoint of their position and velocity. This energy is basically the sum of two others: kinetic energy and potential energy.

KINETIC ENERGY

Objects in motion possess kinetic energy, inasmuch as they are capable of producing movement—that is to say, of moving other bodies.

The magnitude of an object's kinetic energy depends on the object's mass and velocity. The greater the mass and velocity, the greater the kinetic energy.

POTENTIAL ENERGY

is the energy stored in a system, or the energy that the system is capable of delivering. Potential energy is also related to an object's position.

At rest, a stone possesses a given potential energy, which increases if it is suspended above the ground.

The same thing occurs with the ends of a spring when they are pulled apart (the spring stretches, and the potential energy increases).

Kinetic energy is not conserved. Some of it disappears because of the friction of the skis against the snow, but the energy is not lost; it is only transformed into heat.

JULIUS VON MAYER

was born in Germany in 1814. He was a physicist and medical doctor who carried out important work on human metabolism and demonstrated that mechanical work can be transformed into heat, and vice versa. In 1846, he stated the principle of conservation of energy, according to which energy, in a closed system, may be transformed but neither increased nor decreased. He died in 1878.

The Motor of Life

The bonds between the molecules that make up food store energy, which is released during metabolism or combustion. It is the kind of energy that makes living beings "function."

Tigers use chemical energy, which they get from metabolizing food. When they run, part of it is converted into kinetic energy.

90%

is a bicycle's energy efficiency ratio—that is to say, the percentage of energy that is converted into useful work. That of an automobile is only 25 percent.

When the vehicle goes up a slope, its kinetic energy diminishes and is transformed into potential energy—in this case because of the force of gravity.

This potential energy will be released when the vehicle starts down a slope.

Work

The concept of work is closely associated with that of energy. In fact, it can be defined as the amount of energy required to produce the force that moves or deforms an object.

Upon transferring energy to the ball, the soccer player does work.

THE JOULE, THE MEASURE

Work is measured in joules. A joule is the amount of work employed to displace an object by 1 meter with the force of 1 newton.

1 meter

$$1 \text{ joule} = 1\text{kg} \times \frac{\text{m}^2}{\text{s}^2}$$

Meter

Second

The joule is also used to measure the quantity of heat (equivalent to 0.238 calories) and electric energy.

Electric Energy

Many of the forms of work known since the beginning of the 20th century are possible thanks to electric energy. This energy is generated when there is a difference of potential between two points joined by an electric conductor, such as a copper cable.

One of the most common uses of electric energy is lightning. In this case, electric energy is transformed into light and heat.

Lightning, one of the most powerful phenomena in nature, is a manifestation of electric energy, part of which is converted into heat and light.

Batteries store electric energy.

1,000

million volts is the voltage that a bolt of lightning can have.

12,500 kJ

is the average daily energy requirement for an adult male, which is equivalent to some 3,000 calories.

Heat

L ong before the invention of agriculture or writing, people learned to control heat for warmth, for cooking, and for protection from wild animals. More recently, scientists succeeded in explaining the physics of heat and its principles. Heat is associated, at the microscopic level, with the movement of the atoms and molecules that compose matter. It is, furthermore, a form of energy. Heat can be generated by various mechanisms, and it is possible to transmit it through substances, which can do so more or less efficiently. It can be measured; heat energy is commonly expressed in a unit called the calorie. ●

X-Ray of a Push

▶ Fire is synonymous with heat, although properly speaking it is not heat but a form of energy. Heat as a physical phenomenon is determined by the vibration and movement of atoms and molecules (kinetic energy). The greater the kinetic energy, the greater the heat.

The temperature at the surface of the Sun reaches 9,900° F (5,500° C).

Powerful nuclear reactions, which take place in the interior of the Sun, release great quantities of energy in the form of heat.

The Sun consumes 700 million tons of hydrogen per hour and transforms it into helium.

Friction

When two bodies in motion meet, frictional forces convert part of their kinetic energy into heat.

Chemical Reactions

The energy that is stored in molecular bonds may be released in the form of heat during chemical reactions.

Electromagnetic Heat Losses

A large magnet causes molecules with positive and negative charges to vibrate. More vibration equals more kinetic energy and, therefore, more heat.

Heat and Temperature

▶ are related, though different, concepts. Heat is energy, but temperature is only a measure of heat.

Fire heats the air inside the balloon. In other words, energy in the form of heat increases the temperature inside the balloon.

The balloon rises because hot air is less dense than cold air.

136° F (58° C)

was the temperature registered in Al-'Aziziyah (Libya), the highest in history, in 1922.

Measuring Force

Like other forms of energy, heat can be transmitted through different media, although it always fulfills a basic rule: it flows from the warmer medium to the cooler.

1 CONDUCTION

is the way heat is transferred in solids. As the speed at which a molecule vibrates increases, it increases the vibrations of the molecules next to it, and so on.

Metal bar

There are heat conductors that are more or less efficient. Metals, for example, are good conductors. Other materials, such as fiberglass, are so inefficient that they are often used as "insulators."

2 RADIATION

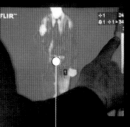

Heat transfer occurs through infrared electromagnetic waves. For example, the heat generated by living beings or by a hot object is transferred to colder surroundings by means of radiation.

A camera capable of detecting infrared emissions shows the emission of heat through radiation.

JAMES P. JOULE

Born in England in 1818, Joule was a physicist and physician who carried out important work on human metabolism and demonstrated that mechanical work can be transformed into heat and vice versa. In 1846, he stated, independently of von Mayer, the principle of conservation of energy, according to which energy, in a closed system, can be transformed but neither increases nor decreases. He died in 1889.

3 CONVECTION

Thermal convection exerts a big influence on the atmosphere and allows us to explain some meteorological processes, such as wind.

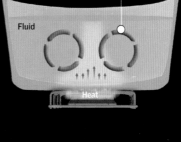

Fluid

Heat

When the medium through which heat is transferred is a fluid, the more energetic (hot) molecules tend to rise above those that are cold or less energetic, creating convection currents that distribute the heat.

Gliders take advantage of rising currents of hot air (convection) to remain in flight without a motor.

The temperature of the corona is over 1.8 million degrees Fahrenheit (1 million degrees C).

Pyrometer

This instrument is used to measure high temperatures greater than 1,000° F (600° C).

Degrees and Calories

Although temperature is measured with the aid of thermometers, which give the values in units such as degrees Celsius or degrees Fahrenheit, heat is measured differently and is typically measured in units called calories.

SCALES

C° Celsius

arises from the division into 100 degrees of the temperature interval between the freezing (0°) and boiling (100°) points of water.

F° Fahrenheit

The concept is similar to that of Celsius degrees, but instead of water, it takes the freezing and boiling points of ammonium chloride in water. The freezing point of water is 32° F.

K° Kelvin

This takes "absolute zero" as its starting point, the temperature at which atoms stop vibrating, which is, in theory, impossible to reach. Absolute zero is equal to -459.67° F (-273.15° C).

Calories

These are used to measure heat—that is to say, they are a measure of energy.

A calorie is defined as the amount of heat necessary to raise the temperature of a gram of water from 58° F (14.5° C) to 60° F (15.5° C) at sea level.

Magnetism

S ome metals, such as iron, have the capacity for generating forces of attraction and repulsion (a characteristic known as magnetism). A "magnetic" object generates a magnetic field around itself with two poles—a positive pole and a negative pole. These poles represent the areas where the maximum force concentrates. Poles with the same sign tend to repel each other, and those with different signs tend to attract each other. This phenomenon has a microscopic origin—it arises from the spin of electrons within atoms—but it has an impact on a big level. In fact, the Earth behaves like a huge magnet. ●

Compass

▶ A compass consists of a magnetized needle that can turn over a horizontal plane marked with the cardinal directions. This needle interacts with the Earth's magnetic field to allow us to estimate the position of the poles.

The Earth's magnetic poles do not coincide with the geographic poles (which mark the axis of the Earth's rotation), although they are very close.

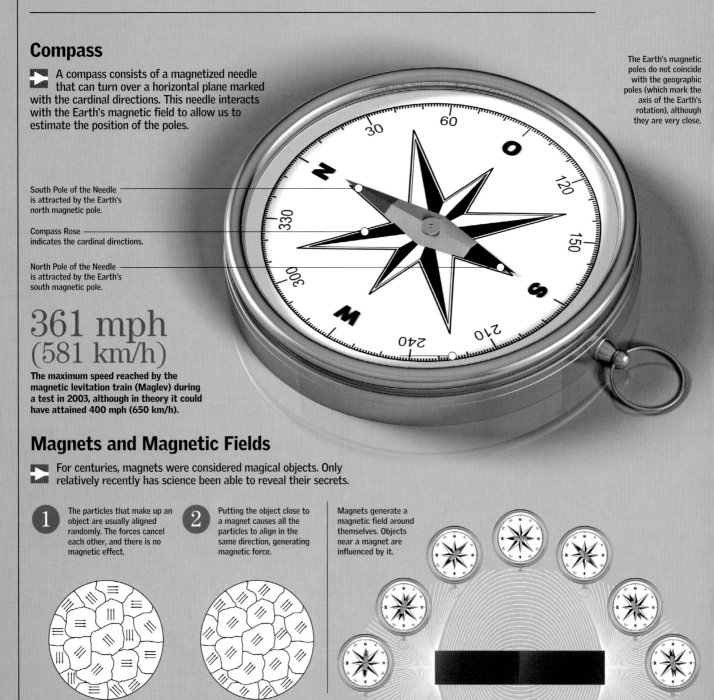

South Pole of the Needle is attracted by the Earth's north magnetic pole.

Compass Rose indicates the cardinal directions.

North Pole of the Needle is attracted by the Earth's south magnetic pole.

361 mph (581 km/h)

The maximum speed reached by the magnetic levitation train (Maglev) during a test in 2003, although in theory it could have attained 400 mph (650 km/h).

Magnets and Magnetic Fields

▶ For centuries, magnets were considered magical objects. Only relatively recently has science been able to reveal their secrets.

1 The particles that make up an object are usually aligned randomly. The forces cancel each other, and there is no magnetic effect.

2 Putting the object close to a magnet causes all the particles to align in the same direction, generating magnetic force.

Magnets generate a magnetic field around themselves. Objects near a magnet are influenced by it.

The Earth, a Huge Magnet

The iron core and the currents of molten rock flowing underneath the Earth's crust generate a magnetic field around the planet. The precise mechanism by which this field is produced continues to be a mystery.

Magnetic Poles

The magnetic poles do not have a fixed, predetermined position. Over time, they continually change position until they end up being completely reversed. During the last 5 million years, more than 20 reversals of the magnetic poles have taken place.

Lines of magnetic force

1,100 miles (1,800 km)

The distance between the magnetic North Pole and the geographic North Pole of the Earth.

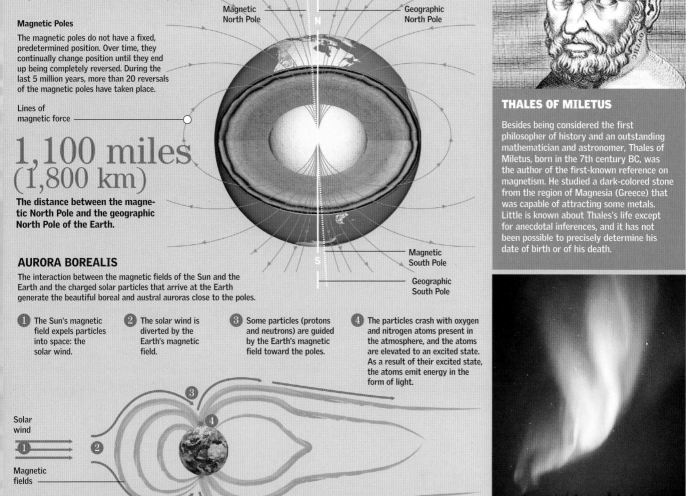

Magnetic North Pole

Geographic North Pole

Magnetic South Pole

Geographic South Pole

AURORA BOREALIS

The interaction between the magnetic fields of the Sun and the Earth and the charged solar particles that arrive at the Earth generate the beautiful boreal and austral auroras close to the poles.

1 The Sun's magnetic field expels particles into space: the solar wind.

2 The solar wind is diverted by the Earth's magnetic field.

3 Some particles (protons and neutrons) are guided by the Earth's magnetic field toward the poles.

4 The particles crash with oxygen and nitrogen atoms present in the atmosphere, and the atoms are elevated to an excited state. As a result of their excited state, the atoms emit energy in the form of light.

Solar wind

Magnetic fields

THALES OF MILETUS

Besides being considered the first philosopher of history and an outstanding mathematician and astronomer, Thales of Miletus, born in the 7th century BC, was the author of the first-known reference on magnetism. He studied a dark-colored stone from the region of Magnesia (Greece) that was capable of attracting some metals. Little is known about Thales's life except for anecdotal inferences, and it has not been possible to precisely determine his date of birth or of his death.

Applications

Since the late 19th century, the phenomenon of magnetism has found countless applications in diverse fields.

ELECTRICITY

The intimate relationship between magnetism and electricity made possible the development of the telephone, the television, the radio, and a great number of electric devices used today.

MEDICINE

Diagnostic methods such as magnetic resonance and computerized axial tomography, which have revolutionized medicine, are based on the principles of magnetism.

CRANES

Cranes with big magnets can lift heavy metallic objects. These magnets are infused with electric current, thanks to the phenomenon known as electromagnetism.

TRANSPORTATION

The magnetic levitation train (Maglev) moves without touching the rails, thanks to the repulsion caused between two opposite magnetic poles. This allows the train to travel at high speeds (greater than 370 mph [600 km/h]).

STORAGE

For some decades now, magnetic tape has been used to record music, videos, and computer files, although this method is now being increasingly replaced by more modern digital systems.

NAVIGATION

For centuries, marine and aerial navigation relied on magnetic compasses. Although magnetic compasses are still widely used, satellite navigation is gaining favor in this field.

Electricity

F ew disruptions to daily life exist that are comparable to a blackout. In the absence of electric lights, a working refrigerator, televisions, desktop computers, or air conditioning—and, in some cases, a functional water pump—a blackout is probably the only time in which we truly stop taking energy for granted and take a moment to realize the importance of one of the most common types of energy in the world. The first person to observe electric energy with scientific precision was Thales of Miletus, in Greece, 27 centuries ago—although he probably was far from imagining the future implications of the phenomenon that drew so much of his interest. ●

BENJAMIN FRANKLIN

Born in 1706, this jack-of-all-trades—one of the most prolific minds in history—is difficult to define. Politician, printer, journalist, inventor: Benjamin Franklin was all of these things and more. Not only was he one of the founding fathers of the United States, but he was also a pioneer in the study of electricity. He is remembered as the scientist behind the famous experiment that demonstrated that lightning is an electric discharge and that clouds are charged with electricity—a discovery he made when he lifted a metal kite during a storm. He was the inventor of the lightning rod, bifocal lenses, and the odometer, among many other things. He died in 1790.

A Question of Electrons

The phenomenon known as electricity originates at the atomic scale and has to do with the behavior and movement of free electrons (electrons separate from the atomic nucleus) in certain media.

Static Electricity

Our practical knowledge of this kind of electricity arises from the unpleasantness and surprise that we get from receiving a small electric shock when we touch a metallic object, a piece of clothing, or even another person's skin under the right circumstances.

Electric Current

Much like water flowing in a river, running freely from one point to another, free electrons flow through conductor materials, such as metals, and manifest themselves in the form of energy, which has numerous useful applications for humankind.

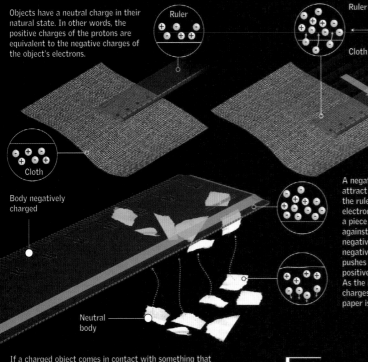

Objects have a neutral charge in their natural state. In other words, the positive charges of the protons are equivalent to the negative charges of the object's electrons.

Ruler

Cloth

Body negatively charged

Cloth

Neutral body

By rubbing an object against another object, electrons from one of the objects flow to the other object. One object provides them, and the other one receives them. Thus, an imbalance is produced. The body that gives away electrons is said to be charged positively, whereas the body that gains electrons is said to be charged negatively.

Ruler

Cloth

A negatively charged body can attract a neutral body. In this case, the ruler is charged (i.e., it receives electrons) by being rubbed against a piece of cloth. Then, when placed against a neutral paper, the negatively charged ruler repels the negative charges of the paper and pushes them away leaving the positive charges on the ruler's side. As the negative and positive charges attract each other, the paper is "attached" to the ruler.

If a charged object comes in contact with something that is in contact with the ground (such as a human body), an electric discharge is produced. In this case, the positively charged finger approaches the metal, which is negatively charged (contains an excess of electrons). If the person is not electrically insulated, he or she functions as a conductor. This is how the unpleasant spark, or shock, is produced.

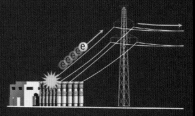

When a difference of potential is applied between the ends of a conductor (for example, a wire), electrons flow, thus generating electric current. This current allows electricity to be transported even at great distances (thousands of miles!) for subsequent distribution and use.

Lightning

Inside stormy clouds, called cumulonimbus clouds, ice particles that are constantly in movement are often electrically charged by friction.

The positively charged particles tend to be located at the upper levels of the cloud.

The negatively charged particles tend to be located at the base of the cloud.

Discharges are produced inside the cloud.

Discharges can be cloud-to-cloud.

48 uninterrupted hours

is the length of time the first electric lightbulb worked. This invention is credited to Thomas Alva Edison, an American scientist, who created it in 1879.

Sometimes a powerful discharge is produced between the base of the cloud, which is negatively charged, and the Earth's surface, which is positively charged and is always ready to receive electrons.

Conductors and Insulators

Materials can be classified as either capable or incapable of conducting electricity. The former show diverse conductivity indexes because not all of them conduct electricity with the same efficiency.

Conductors

Within atoms of conductor materials, electrons are weakly joined with their nucleus. This makes it easy for these electrons to flow as electric energy.

Metals are good conductors because, at an atomic level, the union of the nucleus with the valence electrons is weak. This allows these electrons to flow freely.

Insulator

In insulators, the bond between the nucleus and the electrons of the atoms is strong. For this reason, the flow of electrons is either much more complex or simply does not occur.

600 volts

is the voltage an electric eel can generate during one of its discharges.

Effects of Electricity

As with every form of energy, electricity can be converted to other forms. This is useful for certain applications.

HEAT EFFECT

When an electric current passes through a conductor material, part of the electric energy is converted into heat. This phenomenon is used, quite effectively, in electric heaters.

LIGHT EFFECT

Some solid or gaseous materials produce light as soon as an electric current passes through them.

MAGNETIC EFFECT

Electric currents generate magnetism and vice versa. Two such examples are electromagnetic cranes and magnetic levitation trains.

CHEMICAL EFFECT

Electricity can be used to modify the chemical structure of certain materials. This is the case in electrolysis, which is used to purify elements or to galvanize steel and change it to a less corrosive metal.

Circuits

I n order for electricity to flow and be readily available whenever it is needed at outlets throughout our homes (or each time a device powered by batteries requires it), it is transported by means of a circuit with no breaks or interruptions along the way. Thus, the electric current, produced by an electric generator, travels in a loop. All along this loop, the electric current powers electric devices and encounters diverse mechanisms capable of modifying its characteristics. ●

Back and Forth

Electric circuits can be more or less complex. However, all share certain basic characteristics. Among these basic characteristics are the existence of a source of voltage and electric conductors that help form a circuit.

VOLTAGE SOURCE

It produces electricity from diverse sources (chemical reactions, fossil combustibles, water or air forces, solar energy). In household circuits, electric outlets provide electric energy that is generated in large electric-power plants.

THE POLES

Electric current flows (by convention) from the positive pole to the negative pole.

BATTERIES

are devices that generate electricity from chemical reactions. Excess electrons are produced at one of the terminals, and the other terminal has a deficiency of electrons. In this way, an electric current is produced.

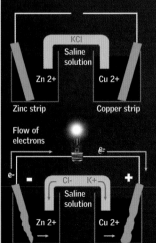

KCl
Saline solution
Zn 2+   Cu 2+
Zinc strip   Copper strip

Flow of electrons
e-   e=
-    Cl-   K+   +
Saline solution
Zn 2+   Cu 2+

ELECTRIC DEVICE

It is powered by the electric current that flows through the circuit.

1,000 volts

is the voltage a circuit can sustain before being considered a high-tension circuit. Some electric power lines transport electricity with voltages up to 350,000 volts.

Direction of the current

CONDUCTORS

The circuit remains closed as long as it is connected by conducting materials.

Direction of the current

RESISTANCE

Any conductor, no matter how efficient it is, presents some resistance to the electric current. The electricity that is supposedly "lost" in the process is, in reality, transformed to heat and light, such as is the case with the filament in a lightbulb. This is the working principle of numerous electric devices, such as heaters and lamps.

THE SWITCH

is a device that is used to interrupt the electric current in a circuit.

ON
OFF

The current is interrupted

The current flows

ON
OFF

Alternating or Direct?

Electric current flows through a conductor in two ways: as alternating current or as direct current.

DIRECT CURRENT

In this type of current, electrons flow in one direction. This type of current is common in electric devices fed by batteries that work at low voltages.

ALTERNATING CURRENT

In this kind of current, the direction of the electrons constantly changes as the polarity of its terminals are repeatedly reversed. Alternating current is the type usually found in households, and it has numerous advantages compared to direct current. Among its most prominent advantages are that it makes it possible to increase or reduce the voltage through the use of a transformer, it can be transported over longer distances with less loss of energy, and it can be used to transmit voices, sounds, and other data.

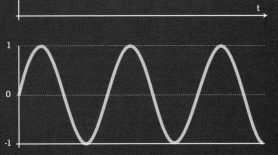

SUPERCONDUCTORS

Because of electric resistance, the transportation of electric energy over long distances results in significant electric charge losses. However, some materials cooled to a temperature close to absolute zero (-273.15° C) begin to have properties of superconductivity—that is, they do not generate resistance, nor, consequently, a loss of energy.

Because of electric resistance in materials, the transportation of electric energy over long distances always results in energy losses.

ELECTRIC POTENTIAL

A terminal that has excess electrons compared with one in which there is a lack of electrons produces a difference in electric potential. The greater the potential difference, the higher the voltage of the electric current. Electric potential is measured in volts.

The voltmeter is a very common tool used to measure the electric potential in a circuit.

50 times per second (50 hertz) **is the rate at which alternating current changes polarity in most homes in the Old World. (Sixty hertz is standard in most of the New World.)**

NIKOLA TESLA

Born in 1856, in what was the Austro-Hungarian Empire, this famous inventor, physicist, and mathematician is remembered for his greatest contribution to science: the alternating current, which succeeded in dethroning the direct-current system, commercialized by Thomas Alva Edison (his commercial rival). Tesla's discovery allowed for the generation, transportation, and use of electric energy on a large scale and over long distances. Additionally, he also succeeded in the first wireless transmission of electromagnetic waves before the experiments carried out by Italian physicist Guglielmo Marconi. Tesla died in 1943.

Electric Units

There are many units for measuring electricity. The following are some of the most common:

AMPERE

Used to measure the strength of an electric current—that is, the quantity of electrons moving through a given part of the circuit per second.

VOLT

Used to measure electric potential—that is, the electromotive force derived from the potential difference between the negative and positive poles in a circuit.

WATT

The power generated from a potential difference of one volt and an electric current of one ampere.

Electric Symbols

In electric or circuit wiring diagrams, certain symbols are used to indicate different components.

Lead wire	
Electric resistance	
Electric battery	
Secondary battery or accumulator	
Electric generator	
Electric motor	
Incandescent bulb	
Switch	
Measuring devices	

Electromagnetism

During the 19th century, scientists discovered that a variable electric current could generate a magnetic field, and that, conversely, a variable magnetic force could generate electricity. The unification of these linked concepts gave birth to the idea of the electromagnetic field, which helped explain the nature of light. It was also the starting point for the development of radio and television, the telephone, and other inventions that have revolutionized people's lives. ●

The Electromagnetic Field

was discovered one-and-a-half centuries ago, through the brilliant intuition of James Clerk Maxwell, a Scottish scientist. This opened up a completely new field of study with surprising and unforeseen applications.

ELECTRICITY CREATES A MAGNETIC FIELD

The Danish physicist Hans Christian Oersted (1777-1851) established that an electric current creates a magnetic field.

A MAGNETIC FIELD CREATES ELECTRICITY

Using Oersted's discoveries as a starting point, Michael Faraday (1791-1867), an English chemist and physicist, discovered that, conversely, a variable magnetic field could also generate an electric current.

Electric current

Lines of magnetic field

Magnet

Magnet

ELECTROMAGNETIC FIELD

The Scottish physicist James Clerk Maxwell (1831-79), having studied these two phenomena, determined that a variable electric current generates a variable electric field, which at the same time generates a variable electric current, and so on. The result is an electromagnetic field indefinitely propagating through space in the form of transverse waves (electromagnetic waves) that travel at the speed of light. This is the basis of wireless communication.

HEINRICH RUDOLF HERTZ

Hertz (1857-94) was a German physicist who, based on the discoveries and experiments of James Clerk Maxwell, established the physical existence of electromagnetic waves and constructed a device that could generate them. He also discovered the photoelectric effect, which Albert Einstein was able to explain years later. In his honor, the unit of frequency in the International System of Units was named the hertz.

Waves

The electromagnetic field propagates in the form of waves, even in a vacuum. Depending on their "size," they have different properties. Some are even visible: we call these visible manifestations of the electromagnetic field *colors*.

WAVES

They are transverse to the direction of propagation. They do not need a material medium to propagate, so they can propagate in vacuum. They travel at the speed of light (300,000 km/s).

WAVELENGTH

is the distance between two consecutive crests. Thus, it shows how "long" the wave is.

FREQUENCY

indicates how many times the wave repeats in a unit of time. Waves of different frequencies have different lengths.

Hertz (Hz)

It is the unit used to measure frequency. One hertz equals one complete cycle of one wave per second.

THE SPECTRUM

is a way to classify waves by their length. Waves of certain wavelengths can be seen as colors.

Beyond the wavelength that corresponds to red lies the infrared band. We cannot see infrared waves, but some animals can.

Spectrum of visible light

Beyond the violet wavelength lies the beginning of the ultraviolet band (a "color" that can be seen by bees, for example).

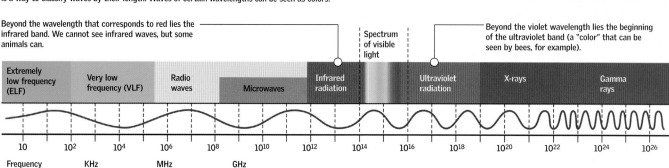

| Extremely low frequency (ELF) | Very low frequency (VLF) | Radio waves | Microwaves | Infrared radiation | Ultraviolet radiation | X-rays | Gamma rays |

| 10 | 10^2 | 10^4 | 10^6 | 10^8 | 10^{10} | 10^{12} | 10^{14} | 10^{16} | 10^{18} | 10^{20} | 10^{22} | 10^{24} | 10^{26} |

Frequency   KHz   MHz   GHz

The Beginning of a Revolution

There are numerous ranges of electromagnetic waves, which have applications in many fields. The following are some of the most notable.

RADIO

interprets variations in the amplitude or in the frequency of waves. These waves contain the information that is transmitted by radio towers.

Carrier wave

AM wave

From a carrier wave, the amplitude to transmit data is modulated. The frequency remains constant.

Carrier wave

FM wave

The frequency of the carrier wave is modulated. The amplitude remains constant. It allows transmissions with higher fidelity, free of atmospheric distortions.

700 nm (nanometer)

is, approximately, the red color's wavelength—that is to say, less than a millionth of a meter.

TELECOMMUNICATIONS

Transmission between cellular telephones and their towers, television broadcasts, and satellite communication are all based on electromagnetic waves.

RADAR

Radars use electromagnetic waves to detect objects in motion, including meteorological conditions inside clouds. They work by sending out waves and analyzing the way in which they are reflected when they strike an object.

X-Rays

Discovered in the 19th century, they revolutionized clinical diagnostic methods. They allow doctors to observe numerous types of body tissue without opening up the patient.

TRANSFORMER

It is used to increase or diminish the voltage of the alternating current. Its invention paved the way for the transportation of large amounts of electricity and of its distribution to the home.

DYNAMO

It transforms mechanical energy into electric energy by means of electromagnetic components. It constitutes the basis of turbines in large electricity generators.

ELECTRIC COIL

It has numerous applications, many of which arise from its ability to store electric energy in the form of a magnetic field. The applications range from igniting a car engine and converting an alternating current into direct current to absorbing sudden changes in voltage.

Sound

A melody, a conversation, an explosion, the murmur of wind through the trees. . . . We are accustomed to thinking of sound as anything that can be heard. However, for physicists, the definition is broader and encompasses a series of special vibrations, only some of which can be perceived by the human ear. Sound consists of vibrations that can alter the solid, liquid, or gaseous medium through which they propagate. In a vacuum, therefore, there can be no sound. ●

The World of Vibrations

▶ Sound can be pictured in the form of waves whose complexity ranges from that of pure sounds (simple waves) to that of impure sounds (compound waves).

FREQUENCY
is the number of times that the wave cycle is repeated each second. The higher the frequency is, the higher the sound's pitch, regardless of the amplitude.

Low-pitched sound

High-pitched sound

AMPLITUDE
represents the intensity of sound. The greater the intensity, the greater the amplitude of the waves. It is usually measured in decibels.

Decibels: 100, 60, 20, 0, -20, -60, -100

Amplitude

Low · Medium · High

The different frequencies and amplitudes of sound from a trumpet

SOUND SPECTRUM
Normally, a sound can be broken down into various waves with frequencies that are multiples of a fundamental frequency, or pure sound. Pure sounds, which are almost nonexistent in nature, are graphed as sinusoidal waves. Pure sounds can be generated by a tuning fork.

Amplitude (Volt): 0.20, 0.15, 0.10, 0.05, 0.00

Frequency (Hz): 0, 500, 1,000, 1,500, 2,000, 2,500

TIMBRE
This is the quality of a sound. It distinguishes the same note played by a piano or a trumpet, for example. It is the result of the number and type of overtones (multiples of the fundamental frequency).

Tuning fork (fundamental frequency)   Flute

Violin   Gong

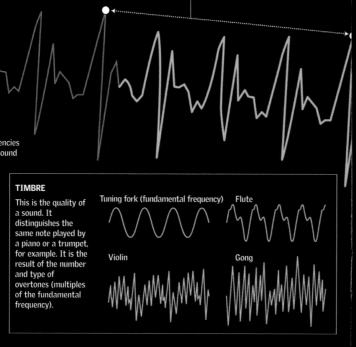

REFLECTION
Sound waves can bounce off certain surfaces. An echo is the best example of this phenomenon. This principle has numerous applications in navigation, topographic surveying, and medicine, among other fields, and it is also used by animals such as bats.

How We Hear

1 When it sounds, the trumpet produces vibrations in the air.

2 The vibrations are transmitted through the molecules of air at 1,115 feet (340 m) per second.

3 The ear picks up the vibrations, which are transmitted through nerves to the brain; this produces the sensation of sound.

100,000 Hz
is the frequency that sounds emitted by bats can reach.

The Speed of Sound

▶ Electromagnetic waves—that is, light, radio, and TV waves, and X-rays—travel at the speed of light, some 186,200 miles (300,000 km) per second. Sound, on the other hand, travels at a notably lower speed, depending on the medium through which it propagates.

In air ———————— 767 mph (1,234 km/h)

In water ———————— 3,355 mph (5,400 km/h)

Through steel ———————— 13,000 mph (21,600 km/h)

MEASURING THE DISTANCE TO A LIGHTNING BOLT

Because of the difference between the speeds of light and sound, we first see the bolt of lightning; thunder, whose sound takes longer to reach us, is heard later. It is possible to calculate the distance to a lightning bolt by measuring the time that elapses between the flash of lightning and the thunder in seconds, and then dividing this number by three to get the distance in kilometers or by five to get the distance in miles.

SONIC BOOM

When an object exceeds the speed of sound, a "sonic boom" is produced. It can be heard when military jets break the "sound barrier."

1 At subsonic speeds, waves travel faster than the airplane. It is therefore possible to hear the sound of the airplane's engines as it approaches.

2 At Mach 1—the speed of sound—the sound waves overlap in front of the airplane.

3 When it exceeds the speed of sound, and, therefore, the overlapping of the waves, a powerful boom is produced. The sound waves are overtaken by the airplane.

Source of Wave

Overlapping

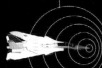

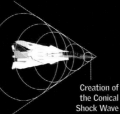

Creation of the Conical Shock Wave

CHUCK YEAGER

was the first man to fly faster than the speed of sound, something that had been attempted before and had cost many lives. Yeager was born in 1923 in Myra, West Virginia, and was a combat pilot during World War II. He succeeded in breaking the sound barrier on October 14, 1947, in an X-1 airplane, when he was flying at an altitude of about 40,000 feet (12,000 m). He retired from the Air Force in 1975 after having broken several aviation records.

Ultrasound

▶ When the frequencies of sound waves are above the limit of human hearing (some 20,000 Hz), they are called ultrasonic waves. Although, logically, it is impossible to hear them, they have numerous applications.

MEDICINE

Uses range from treatments to diagnostic methods. One of the best-known applications of ultrasound is sonography, which can be used to study internal injuries and the status of a pregnancy.

INDUSTRY

With ultrasound, materials can be analyzed without destroying them, and different tests can be performed on them. It can also produce emulsions of liquid and oily substances.

ECHOLOCATION

Sonar, the navigational instrument of submarines, functions somewhat like radar, but instead of electromagnetic waves it emits sound pulses. In nature, some animals, such as bats and dolphins, produce ultrasonic pulses to locate their prey or to evade obstacles.

W e arrive home at night, and we turn on the lights. Electric current reaches the lightbulb, and, as if by magic, it lights up. Now we can see all the objects that surround us—not only their forms but also their colors. But, what is light? Why do things have different colors? This question took centuries to be answered. Today we know that it is a form of energy, of electromagnetic radiation, which can behave both as a wave and as a particle called a photon. ●

The Wavy Nature of Light

▶ According to the most accepted theories, light is made up of energetic particles called photons. The energy level of these particles and their wavelength determine color.

WHITE LIGHT

Light that comes from the Sun is composed of a mixture of lights of various wavelengths. This light can be broken down with the aid of a prism.

PRISMS

Because each wavelength (each color) has a different index of refraction, each is deflected by the prism at a different angle. That is why it is possible to "separate" colors.

Violin

Refraction

▶ One of the most notable phenomena of light is that of refraction. It is a result of the changes in speed that light undergoes when it passes through media of different natures.

Light travels at different speeds in air and in water, and, therefore, when it passes from one medium to another, it is deflected. That is why a pencil submerged in water will give the impression of being broken.

Materials have different indexes of refraction, just as there are different indexes for different wavelengths.

Reflection

▶ Rays of light can be reflected by objects. We encounter this phenomenon all around us. If the reflecting surface is smooth, then it reflects light in a single direction.

MIRRORS

The smooth and polished surface of a mirror demonstrates the Law of Reflection. This law says that the angle formed when a ray hits the surface of a mirror is equal to the angle formed by the reflected ray.

Smooth Surface

Optical Illusions

▶ Vision is the result not only of the nature of light but also the way in which the eye perceives it—hence the phenomenon of optical illusions.

Instead of all being the same, the stripes in the French naval flag are each a different size, in the ratio 30:33:37. This way, fluttering over the sea, the stripes all appear to be the same.

| 30 | 33 | 37 |

Although it is hard to believe, the horizontal lines in these squares are parallel.

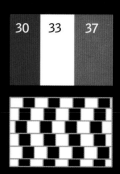

What Are Colors?

Within the electromagnetic spectrum, we are able to "see" electromagnetic waves of different sizes. Our brain produces the sensation of color, according to the wavelengths of these waves. Each color corresponds to a specific wavelength.

THE SPECTRUM	COLOR	Wavelength	Frequency
Our eyes are able to see part of the electromagnetic spectrum: the part between the waves corresponding to red and those corresponding to violet.	Red	~ 625-740 nm	~ 480-405 THz
	Orange	~ 590-625 nm	~ 510-480 THz
	Yellow	~ 565-590 nm	~ 530-510 THz
	Green	~ 520-565 nm	~ 580-530 THz
	Blue	~ 450-500 nm	~ 670-600 THz
	Indigo	~ 430-450 nm	~ 700-670 THz
	Violet	~ 380-430 nm	~ 790-700 THz

When an object illuminated by white light reflects the wavelength corresponding to red, we perceive it as a red object.

When it reflects all wavelengths, we see it as white.

When it reflects no wavelengths, we see it as black.

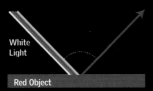

White Light

Red Object

CHRISTIAAN HUYGENS

was a physicist, astronomer, and mathematician born in The Hague in 1629. In addition to being a skilled telescope maker and having discovered the rings of Saturn with one of his telescopes, Huygens formulated the wave theory of light. This theory stood in opposition to the theory formulated by Isaac Newton, who believed that light was made up of small, shining bodies (science later discovered that both theories were partly correct). Huygens died in 1695.

SPF

This is the abbreviation for "sun protection factor." In sunscreens, it indicates how long one can be exposed to the Sun without burning; to determine the approximate number of minutes of protection, one can multiply one's normal safe period by the SPF. For example, someone who normally burns in 20 minutes would burn in 240 minutes (4 hours) wearing an SPF 12 sunscreen.

"Invisible" Colors

Beyond red and violet, the limits of the spectrum that we can see, there are other "colors" invisible to our eyes, although they are visible to some animals. There are numerous applications for these parts of the spectrum by means of cameras and special filters.

INFRARED

Because plant chlorophyll is perceptible by infrared, the deforestation of the Amazon can be seen in this satellite image.

Heat emits in infrared. Thus, an infrared camera makes it possible to take the temperature of the ocean and atmosphere, as in the case of the "thermal" image of this hurricane, in which the red areas correspond to warmer regions and the blue to cooler regions.

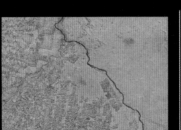

ULTRAVIOLET

Ultraviolet rays are part of the solar radiation that reaches the Earth and are what produces a tan after sunbathing.

Black Light

is a type of lightbulb that emits ultraviolet waves and very little visible light, producing surprising effects. They are sometimes used in concerts, theaters, and homes for illuminating special paints.

Certain substances invisible to our eyes begin to fluoresce under ultraviolet light. This is the case with blood, for example, which makes this type of technique especially important in forensic technology.

Special Relativity

U ntil the beginning of the 20th century, a physicist's understanding of how the world worked was based on the laws proposed by Isaac Newton. However, these laws could not explain certain experimental results. A young 25-year-old German-born physicist named Albert Einstein then appeared on the scene and shook the foundations of classical physics with his insight into the universe. ●

Background

Scientists at the beginning of the 20th century believed that any physical phenomenon could be explained through Newtonian mechanics and that electromagnetic phenomena could be explained with Maxwell's equations. They did not imagine that a new integrated vision of physics would even be remotely necessary.

ACCORDING TO THIS PRE-EINSTEIN MODEL

Time
was an absolute value; thus, a second had the same intrinsic and absolute value anywhere in the universe.

Space
was also considered an absolute value.

Light
propagated in the form of waves through a medium called the "light ether," although nobody had been able to detect this exotic medium.

Ether
was believed to be the uniform and motionless parameter of a universe in motion.

A Failure That Opened the Door to New Ideas

In 1887, physicists Albert A. Michelson and Edward W. Morley carried out an experiment to estimate the "absolute movement" of the Earth. They wanted to compare the planet's movement in relation to the ether that supposedly permeated all of outer space in an "absolute motionless state" of rest. They undertook this experiment because they believed that they had found a method capable of detecting the ether.

1 A light ray is split into two beams that are emitted in two different directions: one in the direction in which the Earth is traveling and the other perpendicular to it.

2 The ether should have a different effect on each beam because of the different directions that each beam is traveling. Therefore, the beams should return to the receptor slightly out of phase.

3 The experiment was a failure, however, because the emitted beams always, within the limits of experimental error, returned in phase.

Light emitter

299,792,458

meters per second
is the speed of light in a vacuum; the meter is now defined as the exact distance that light travels in a vacuum in 1/299,792,458 of a second (the meter is redefined whenever a more precise measurement is made).

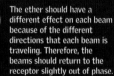

Mirror

Prism

Mirror

Receptor

Lorentz's Contraction

In order to explain the negative result of the Michelson-Morley experiment, physicist George F. FitzGerald proposed that objects in movement suffer compression. For that reason, a light beam pointed in the direction of the Earth's movement will travel a shorter distance than a perpendicular beam. This, in theory, compensated for the ether effect. Thus, according to FitzGerald's calculations,

SPEED	THE OBJECT SHRINKS
11.2 km/s (speed of a rocket)	2 parts per billion
262,000 km/s	50%
300,000 km/s (speed of light)	100% (object length = 0)

Based on FitzGerald's contraction hypothesis, a Dutch physicist named Hendrik A. Lorentz proposed that a shrinking charge increases its mass. Thus, according to Lorentz's calculations,

SPEED	INCREASE IN MASS
149,000 km/s	15%
262,000 km/s	100% (mass is doubled)
300,000 km/s (speed of light)	Infinite mass

The Einstein Revolution

In his Special Theory of Relativity, published in 1905, Albert Einstein proposed a revolutionary solution for the problems concerning the ether. His theory consists of two postulates.

FIRST POSTULATE

No reference system can be considered at rest in the universe (nothing is motionless) nor can absolute measurements be made. Measurements depend on the observer, and they differ according to the state in which we find the observer. .

Einstein also established that all of the laws of physics apply equally to different observers who are moving at a uniform speed with respect to each other. Later, in his General Theory of Relativity, Einstein extended the applications of this theory to any reference system, independent of its movement.

SECOND POSTULATE

The only constant value in the universe is the speed of light in a vacuum, independent of the fact that its source is at rest or in motion.

According to Newtonian, or classical physics, the speed of light that a locomotive in motion emits should be equal to the speed of light added to the speed of the locomotive.

Einstein states that, regardless of the movement or lack of movement of the source of light, the speed of light is always constant. Because speed equals the ratio between distance and time, this means that space and time are not absolute values but can vary.

Is a human being big or small? Compared to an average dog, an average human being is big. However, this same average human is small when standing next to an elephant. In other words, a human being's size is relative to the observer or the system of reference.

If an object is thrown from a locomotive in motion, the final speed of the object is determined by adding the speed of the locomotive to the speed at which it is thrown.

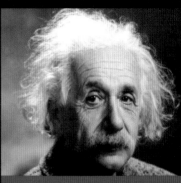

ALBERT EINSTEIN

was the scientific icon of the 20th century, and his theory changed our vision of the universe. He was born in Germany, in 1879, and became a U.S. citizen through naturalization in 1940. When he was only 25 years old, while serving as an employee in a patent office in Switzerland, he published the Special Theory of Relativity, which 10 years later was complemented by the General Theory of Relativity. In 1921, he received the Nobel Prize for Physics, not for his theory of relativity but rather for his explanation of the photoelectric effect. He was persecuted by the Nazis for being a Jew, which forced him to immigrate to the United States, where he died in 1955. At the time of his death, he was still very intellectually active and working on mathematical equations to join the four fundamental forces of the universe.

$$E = mc^2$$

The most famous mathematical equation in the world was postulated by Einstein. It equates energy to mass, because, according to Einstein, they are equivalent concepts. This equation inspired humankind to harness nuclear power.

Clocks That Run Late

One of the most impressive consequences of Einstein's theory is that time runs at different speeds, depending on whether an object is at rest or is in motion. This happens because time is a relative, not an absolute, value.

1 A hypothetical spaceship traveling at 163,000 miles/second (262,000 km/s) approaches a similar spaceship that is at rest.

2 The astronaut in motion does not notice any change in the speed of his clock inside his spaceship.

3 But the astronaut in the craft at rest observes that inside the spaceship in motion time passes half as fast as on the clock inside his spacecraft at rest. In addition the approaching spaceship has twice the mass and is half the size of his spaceship at rest.

4 One hour later, the spaceship in motion comes to a stop. It recovers its size and mass, but its clock shows a delay of half an hour in relation to its counterpart clock inside the ship that was at rest.

Clock inside the spaceship in motion

Clock inside the spaceship at rest

In 1971 this "thought experiment" was verified.

First, high-precision atomic clocks were synchronized.

Then, some of them were mounted in a commercial aircraft and flown for 40 hours.

When they returned to Earth, the clocks were no longer synchronized—just as Einstein had predicted!

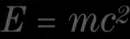

General Relativity

W hen the world learned of the revolutionary Special Theory of Relativity proposed by Albert Einstein and published in 1905, physics underwent its most revolutionary change since the days of Isaac Newton. Nevertheless, Einstein had yet another surprise left: the so-called General Theory of Relativity, of 1916—a much more complex and complete theory from which several interesting predictions arise and have been confirmed over time. ●

Why a Second Theory?

➤ According to Einstein, the Special Theory of Relativity was incomplete because it only applied to inertial systems (in uniform motion) and not to accelerated systems. The problem was that all bodies in the universe, according to classical, or Newtonian, physics, are subject to acceleration forces caused by their mutual gravitational attractions. Einstein solved the problem of generalizing his theory by postulating the equivalence principle.

A Deformed Universe

➤ Einstein established that gravity was not a force, but rather the consequence of the deformation of space-time that any body with mass generates. Thus, when approaching a planet, for example, an object is not attracted by any force, but it travels through that curved deformation.

This novel interpretation of gravity allowed Einstein to accurately make spectacular predictions relating to the force of gravity.

Emisor de luz

Light That Bends

➤ Perhaps the most impressive confirmation of one of Einstein's predictions, based on the General Theory of Relativity, happened in 1919, during the course of a solar eclipse.

According to the General Theory of Relativity, gravitational fields bend light rays. Einstein predicted that a light ray that barely touches the Sun's surface would be diverted 1.75 seconds of arc, which could be measured by observing the image of a distant star near the edge of the Sun. Therefore, the world had to wait for an eclipse before this effect could be confirmed.

In 1919, during a solar eclipse, scientists were able to confirm that the image of stars near the Sun appeared to have shifted with respect to their normal positions.

Real position of the star

Sun

Earth

Apparent position of the star

4

The universe has four dimensions, according to Einstein's vision, although the fourth (time) behaves differently from the other three (length, width, and height).

Gravitational Lenses

➡️ Another prediction based on the General Theory of Relativity concerns gravitational lenses. Because of this phenomenon, which is also related to the space-time deformation caused by gravity, the image of certain far stars and galaxies is deformed when seen from the Earth.

Normal trajectory of light ➡️➡️

Trajectory of light

Distant galaxy

Earth

Imaginary line

Diverted light as a result of gravity

The objects that are very massive (with great gravitational fields) work much the same way as optical lenses.

If an object is thrown forward from a moving train, the object's final speed can be calculated by adding the speed with which it was thrown to the speed at which the train is traveling.

Astronomers can use the effect of gravitational lenses to find objects that do not emit light or that are undetectable for other reasons.

HENDRIK A. LORENTZ

The vision and contributions that this great Dutch physicist and mathematician, born in 1853, made to the field of classical physics greatly helped the development of the relativity theories of Einstein. Lorentz's equations developed along the lines of those of George F. FitzGerald. They demonstrate how a body changes its shape and mass because of its motion. This became one of the pillars of Einstein's theories, although from Lorentz's perspective they merely constituted one more contribution to physics of the many he had proposed. In 1902, he was awarded the Nobel Prize for Physics. He died in 1928.

Electromagnetic Waves

➡️ Einstein theorized that an intense gravitational field could restrain the vibrations of atoms. In other words, this would make them lose energy. Because waves "stretch" when losing energy (that is, they become redder), this effect would cause a redshift in the electromagnetic wave.

This experiment was carried out by analyzing the spectrum of dwarf stars, and the predicted redshift was confirmed.

Perturbation of Mercury's Orbit

➡️ Astronomers had discovered a discrepancy in the expected position of the planet Mercury that could not be explained by Newtonian, or classical, physics without inventing some hypothetical planet. Einstein used his theory to explain the discrepancy, eliminating the problem of the missing planet.

For years, astronomers looked for a hypothetical planet called Vulcan, which would be responsible for the perturbations of Mercury's orbit.

However, Einstein explained that the perturbations were the result of the deformation of space-time produced by the Sun, and he proved this with precise equations. This phenomenon occurs with all planets, but it is more noticeable in Mercury's orbit because of its proximity to the Sun.

76 years

was Albert Einstein's age when he died, in Princeton, New Jersey.

Quantum Mechanics

J ust as scientists discovered, at the beginning of the 20th century, that the laws of the until-then untouchable Newtonian physics (classic physics) did not apply to objects with great mass and velocity (a discovery which would open the door for the development of the theory of relativity), they also realized that these same laws of classical physics did not apply at an atomic or subatomic scale either. A new theory—quantum mechanics—arose that could explain, or at least provide a glimpse of, the functioning of the minutest physical elements of the universe.

Clouds Replace Points

To estimate the position or movement of a car or a star is easy. However, at an atomic scale, things become much more complicated. According to quantum mechanics, we are incapable of measuring such properties as the speed and position of an electron without disturbing it.

WHERE IS THE ELECTRON?

IN CLASSICAL PHYSICS

In order to represent an atom in a specific moment, for example, it was enough to show an atomic nucleus and the electrons that spin around such nucleus in a predetermined position.

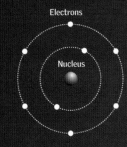

Electrons

Nucleus

IN QUANTUM MECHANICS

Because it is impossible to establish the exact position of electrons, atoms are represented by their probable positions. At the right, a hydrogen atom is shown with the cloud of probabilities for the location of its only electron.

According to the "Heisenberg Uncertainty Principle," it is not possible to measure the speed of a particle without disturbing its position or to measure the position of a particle without modifying its speed.

1,000

atoms can form a mesoscopic system (between the macroscopic scale that surrounds us and the atomic scale) that shows the effects of the quantum laws.

Quantum

Quantum mechanics was born thanks to a discovery made by the German physicist Max Planck, who established that energy is not a continuous value but rather is transmitted in the form of small packages, or "quanta."

A quantum is the smallest unit of energy. In other words, a quantum is to energy what an atom is to matter.

Waves or Particles?

▶ Quantum mechanics postulates that particles, in certain conditions, can behave as small particles or as waves.

Light is a good example of the wave-particle duality. Light can be transmitted as a flow of discontinuous particles (photons) or in continuous form, as a wave. In the latter case, waves have probabilistic properties, as if photons were dispersed throughout the wave.

Photons

Continuous waves

Photons

was the year in which Max Planck postulated that energy could be transmitted in the form of quanta.

STM

is the acronym of Scanning Tunneling Microscope, a device used to carry out research at a subatomic level and whose tip is one atom thick.

The "Tunneling Effect"

▶ is another way in which matter behaves at an atomic scale and for which there is no comparable behavior at larger scales.

According to classical physics, a particle with a certain energy cannot cross a barrier of greater energy.

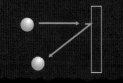

According to quantum mechanics, on the other hand, the probability that the particle can be found on the other side of the barrier is not null, and consequently it is possible that the particle can cross it.

The tunneling effect is used in a type of microscope used to "see" atoms. It also helps to explain atomic fusion in stars at theoretically low temperatures.

MAX PLANCK

was a German physicist, born in 1858, who established the foundation of quantum mechanics when he found a way to explain how energy is transmitted. This happened while he was experimenting with radiation; his experiments did not agree with the expected results. Planck then theorized that energy was not transmitted in a continuous way, as had been believed up until that time, but in the form of small packages (quanta). This observation led to the birth of quantum mechanics. Plank received a Nobel Prize for Physics in 1918. He died in 1947.

Quantum Computer

The data-processing capacity of computers doubles approximately every two years, whereas their components keep getting smaller. However, this tendency has a limit. In order for this trend to continue, computers soon will require atomic-sized components (a scale at which the laws of classic physics stop working, and matter responds to rules of quantum mechanics). At that point, transistors will be obsolete. If scientists manage to overcome this challenge, we will have a processor that is millions of times faster than the ones we currently have. ●

"Qubits" Arrive

The operation of today's computers is based on bits (the most elementary unit of information storage). Quantum computers will store their information in qubits.

BITS

Today computer information is stored in bits. In order to make a bit, one first needs to make a physical device that is capable of adopting the binary system inherent to a bit: for example, "zero" or "one," "true" or "false," "on" or "off."

This physical device has the limitation that it can only adopt one of these binary values at a time. In today's computers, miniature transistors and capacitors carry out this work.

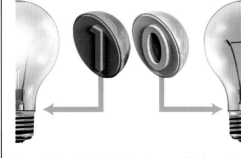

A record of three bits at a given time in a conventional computer can be represented this way.

The same record, but with three qubits (quantum computation), at a given time results in eight values, thanks to quantum superposition.

20 minutes

is the time it could take a quantum computer to factor a 1,000-digit number. A conventional computer, on the other hand, could take several billion years to make this same calculation.

THE QUBIT

According to the laws of quantum mechanics, particles can adopt the state of both a wave and particle at the same time, with an infinite number of intermediate states (something inconceivable in classical physics). It can be represented as a point in a sphere, in which the north pole is equivalent to "one," and the south pole to "zero." This phenomenon is called "quantum superposition." Through quantum superposition, three qubits can be used to represent up to eight values (2^3) simultaneously—an ordinary computer could only represent one of those eight values at a time. ——

When a qubit has to carry out a measurement, it must define itself as a "zero" or as a "one." This depends on a series of probabilities, according to its position.

Just like a bit, the qubit eventually acquires a certain value. The difference lies in capacity and calculation speed.

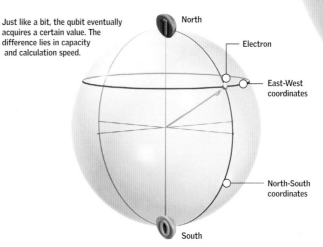

North

Electron

East-West coordinates

North-South coordinates

South

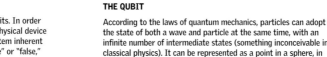

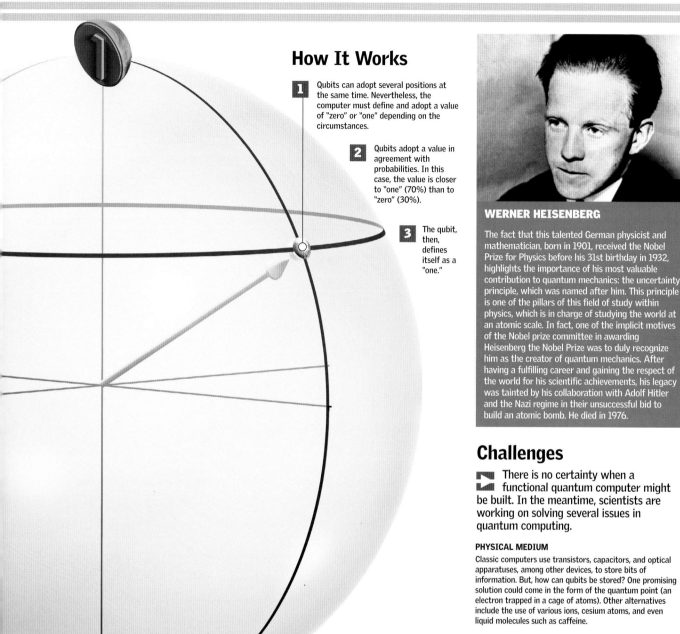

How It Works

1 Qubits can adopt several positions at the same time. Nevertheless, the computer must define and adopt a value of "zero" or "one" depending on the circumstances.

2 Qubits adopt a value in agreement with probabilities. In this case, the value is closer to "one" (70%) than to "zero" (30%).

3 The qubit, then, defines itself as a "one."

WERNER HEISENBERG

The fact that this talented German physicist and mathematician, born in 1901, received the Nobel Prize for Physics before his 31st birthday in 1932, highlights the importance of his most valuable contribution to quantum mechanics: the uncertainty principle, which was named after him. This principle is one of the pillars of this field of study within physics, which is in charge of studying the world at an atomic scale. In fact, one of the implicit motives of the Nobel prize committee in awarding Heisenberg the Nobel Prize was to duly recognize him as the creator of quantum mechanics. After having a fulfilling career and gaining the respect of the world for his scientific achievements, his legacy was tainted by his collaboration with Adolf Hitler and the Nazi regime in their unsuccessful bid to build an atomic bomb. He died in 1976.

Challenges

There is no certainty when a functional quantum computer might be built. In the meantime, scientists are working on solving several issues in quantum computing.

PHYSICAL MEDIUM

Classic computers use transistors, capacitors, and optical apparatuses, among other devices, to store bits of information. But, how can qubits be stored? One promising solution could come in the form of the quantum point (an electron trapped in a cage of atoms). Other alternatives include the use of various ions, cesium atoms, and even liquid molecules such as caffeine.

INTERFERENCE

In theory, the number of qubits that a computer can have is infinite, but in reality a few qubits working together begin to undergo external interference (from such sources as radiation or cosmic rays) and even start to interfere with themselves.

ERRORS

Bits are categorical. One bit can be a "one" or a "zero." But qubits work through probabilities. If the value of a qubit is very close or equal to 50 percent, then errors will undoubtedly be produced, which, when accumulated, could generate untrustworthy results.

28 qubits

is the number of qubits used by the largest quantum processor built to date, according to its developer D-Wave Systems. However, the experimental system is just beginning to reach the level of practical applications.

Applications

CALCULATIONS IN PARALLEL

One of the major capabilities of quantum computers would be their capacity to accurately carry out astronomical numbers of calculations in only one circuit (for factorization and computation of exponents). They would be, without a doubt, very tough rivals in a chess match.

SECURITY

The capability of quantum computers to encrypt data would make even the most advanced systems today obsolete.

TELEPORTATION

This concept is not to be confused with the teletransportation portrayed in science fiction: matter and energy cannot be transported in this way. In quantum computing, teleportation refers to the transmission at a distance of the quantum state of an atom, which could be useful, for example, in the field of telecommunications.

SEARCHES

Quantum computers and qubits will reduce the time it takes to carry out data searches.

VERIFICATION OF THEOREMS

Currently, some mathematical theorems are unverifiable because of the massive number of calculations they require. Quantum computers could solve this.

Uses and Applications

WIND ENERGY
Wind is one of the most promising renewable resources. Many countries take advantage of the wind's force to generate electricity or to pump water.

E arly humans relied on their own brute force and the energy supplied by animals. Later, humans discovered coal and petroleum (along with another hydrocarbon, natural gas). Petroleum reserves are finite and increasingly in demand around the world, however. In addition, petroleum extraction and

SOURCES OF ENERGY 68-69

PETROLEUM 70-71

NATURAL GAS 72-73

HYDROELECTRIC ENERGY 74-75

NUCLEAR ENERGY 76-77

SOLAR ENERGY 78-79

WIND ENERGY 80-81

BIOFUELS 82-83

BIODIGESTORS 84-85

GEOTHERMAL ENERGY 86-87

TIDAL ENERGY 88-89

HYDROGEN 90-91

combustion produce pollution. For all these reasons, humans have experimented with alternative sources of energy. Some are clean but are not very efficient. Others are inexhaustible, efficient, and "green," but are very expensive. In the following chapter, you will discover how each of these new alternative energy sources works, as well as their advantages and disadvantages. ●

Sources of Energy

S ince the invention of the steam engine, humans have relied more and more on nonrenewable sources of energy, especially coal, petroleum, and natural gas—the reserves of which are limited. To a lesser extent they have made use of renewable resources, such as water power from rivers to produce electricity, that nevertheless come at a cost to the environment. Thus, one of the greatest challenges of today is how to obtain energy in an economical, safe, and clean way from renewable sources. ●

Clean or Not

Besides the importance of availability, the impact that sources of energy produce on the environment counts a great deal.

WORLDWIDE PRODUCTION OF ENERGY

Petroleum	35.0%
Coal	25.3%
Natural Gas	20.7%
Biofuel, Renewable Fuels, and Garbage	10.0%
Nuclear Energy	6.3%
Hydroelectric Energy	2.2%
Other	0.5%

USEFUL GARBAGE

Organic waste can be treated in biodigestors to produce heat, electricity, and fertilizers.

THE HEAT OF THE EARTH

Geothermal plants take advantage of energy in the form of heat that exists beneath the Earth's crust, especially in volcanic areas, to produce electric energy.

WIND ENERGY

One of the most promising sources of future energy is wind energy that, little by little, has come to be regarded as a feasible energy alternative. Clean, unlimited, and economical, it basically only requires a location with wind to turn the blades of large wind turbines. Its critics point to its negative impact on the landscape.

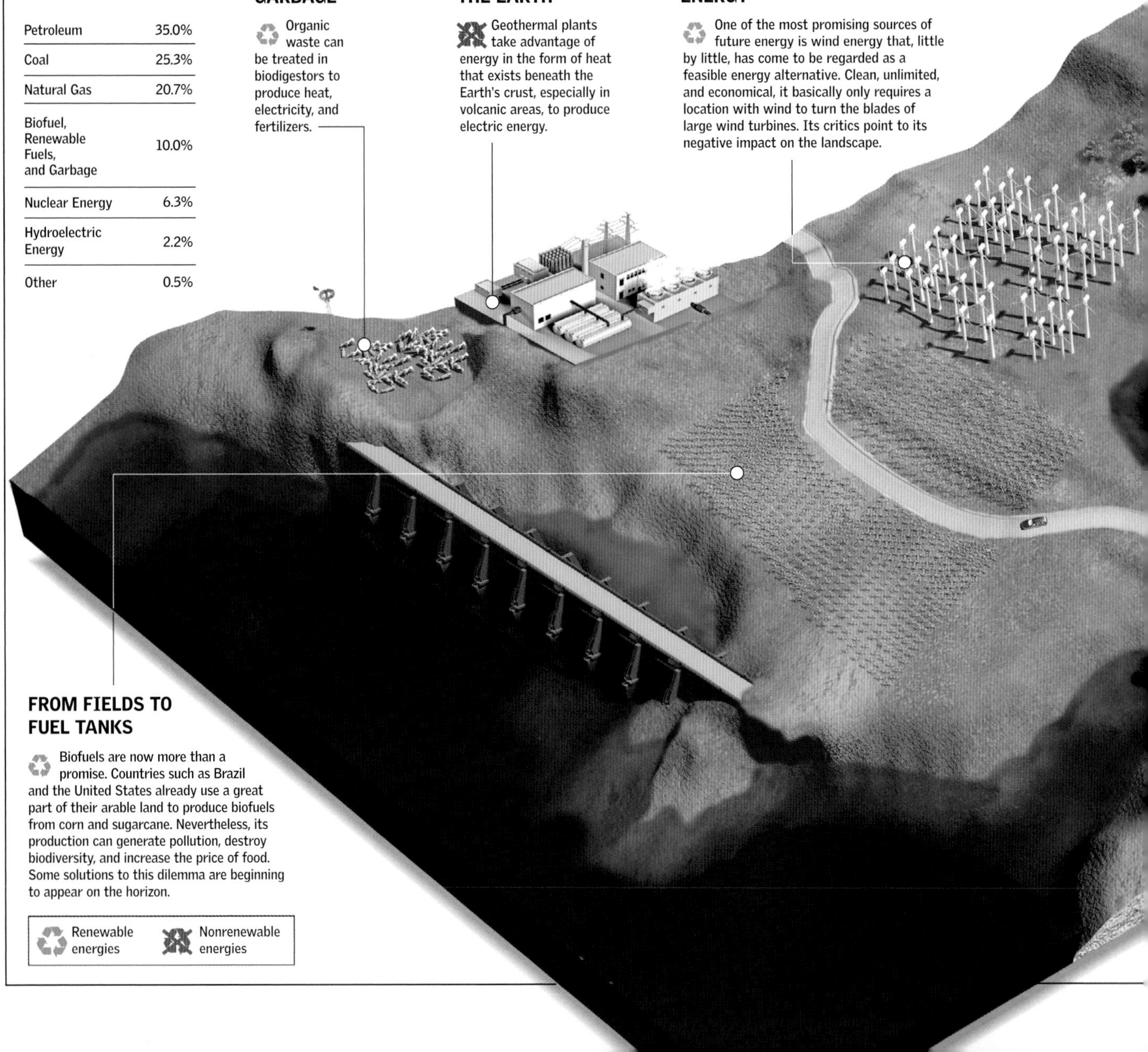

FROM FIELDS TO FUEL TANKS

Biofuels are now more than a promise. Countries such as Brazil and the United States already use a great part of their arable land to produce biofuels from corn and sugarcane. Nevertheless, its production can generate pollution, destroy biodiversity, and increase the price of food. Some solutions to this dilemma are beginning to appear on the horizon.

Renewable energies		Nonrenewable energies	

THE GIFT OF SUNSHINE

Decades ago, humans began to use solar energy to produce electricity and heat. However, even though today all types of solar devices exist, from calculators to airplanes, this inexhaustible and clean energetic source has not been able to overcome two great limitations: its low efficiency and its high cost.

THE ART OF TAMING WATER

Human talent and creativity has managed to turn the great forces that drive rivers into cheap, clean, and endless electricity. Hydroelectric dams are in operation in many different places. Some have truly extraordinary dimensions. However, their negative impact on the environment is not often taken into account.

11,435

million tons of petroleum is the equivalent annual worldwide production of energy, according to the latest estimate from 2005. It was approximately half of that 30 years ago.

NUCLEAR ENERGY: THE MOST CONTROVERSIAL SOURCE

It is perhaps the most efficient: a clean source, powerful, and almost unlimited. However, it requires great capital investment and the handling of complex technologies, and it carries a disquieting risk of a nuclear accident. In addition, it generates toxic and highly dangerous residues.

12.9%

of the worldwide petroleum supply is produced by Saudi Arabia, followed by Russia (12.1%), the United States (7.9%), and Iran (5.5%).

BLACK GOLD AND NATURAL GAS

By far, hydrocarbons are the source of energy of choice in most countries. Although they constitute an abundant and economical source of energy, their reserves are limited, and their consumption on a massive scale contributes to the greenhouse effect and global warming.

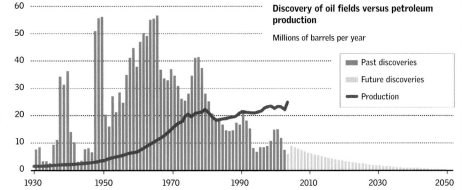

Discovery of oil fields versus petroleum production

Millions of barrels per year

- Past discoveries
- Future discoveries
- Production

Petroleum

P etroleum is the main energy source in the developed world. It comes from ancient organic deposits that have been buried in the bowels of the Earth for hundreds of millions of years. Its pure state, called crude oil, is a mix of different hydrocarbons of little use, and hence the oil must first be distilled to separate its components. This valuable resource, which pollutes the atmosphere when burned, is nonrenewable and available only in limited reserves; these characteristics have driven researchers to look for alternative energy sources. ●

Contaminant-gas treatment units

From the Well to the Tank

 After its extraction, crude oil is distilled and fractioned into several products, among them gasoline.

Gas flare stack

2 CRUDE OIL STORAGE
The crude oil is stored and then transported to refineries through pipelines or by large tanker ships.

1 EXTRACTION
The oil is pumped from the deposit up to the storage tanks.

3 VAPORIZATION
The crude oil is heated in a boiler up to 752° F (400° C) or more. Once vaporized, it is sent through the distilling tower.

2050

The year the world's oil reserves could run out if the current rate of consumption is maintained and no new discoveries are made.

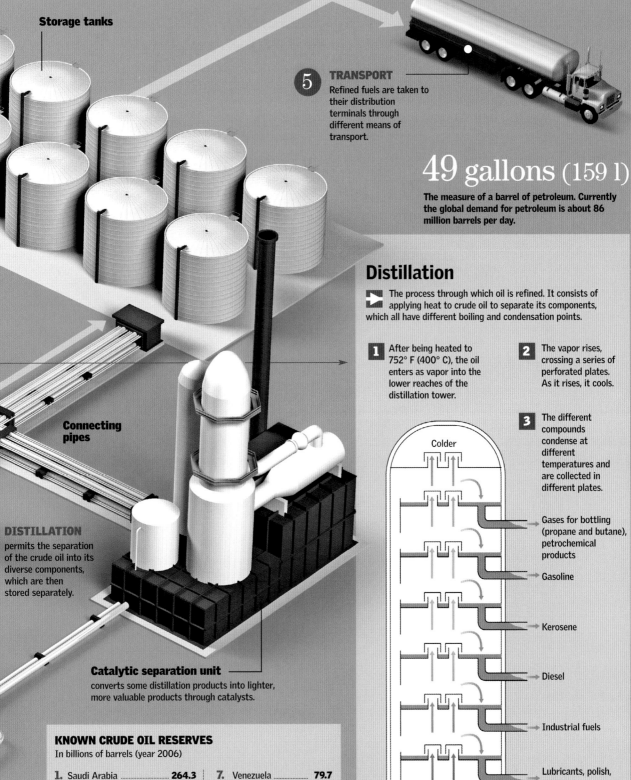

Storage tanks

5 **TRANSPORT**
Refined fuels are taken to their distribution terminals through different means of transport.

49 gallons (159 l)

The measure of a barrel of petroleum. Currently the global demand for petroleum is about 86 million barrels per day.

Distillation

The process through which oil is refined. It consists of applying heat to crude oil to separate its components, which all have different boiling and condensation points.

1 After being heated to 752° F (400° C), the oil enters as vapor into the lower reaches of the distillation tower.

2 The vapor rises, crossing a series of perforated plates. As it rises, it cools.

3 The different compounds condense at different temperatures and are collected in different plates.

Connecting pipes

4 **DISTILLATION**
permits the separation of the crude oil into its diverse components, which are then stored separately.

Catalytic separation unit
converts some distillation products into lighter, more valuable products through catalysts.

Residual treatment system

Colder

Gases for bottling (propane and butane), petrochemical products

Gasoline

Kerosene

Diesel

Industrial fuels

Lubricants, polish, waxes

Asphalt, waterproofing, other residues

Gasified crude oil   Hotter

KNOWN CRUDE OIL RESERVES
In billions of barrels (year 2006)

1. Saudi Arabia	264.3	7. Venezuela	79.7
2. Canada	178.8	8. Russia	60.0
3. Iran	132.5	9. Libya	39.1
4. Iraq	115.0	10 Nigeria	35.9
5. Kuwait	101.5	11. United States	21.4
6. United Arab Emirates	97.8	Rest of the world	166.6

Natural Gas

A fter petroleum, natural gas slowly rose to a position of importance in the global balance of energy sources because of its availability and efficiency. It has a reputation of being the cleanest fossil fuel. Technological advances, especially in the discovery of deposits, have produced an explosion in the reserve statistics in the last 15 years. These developments have been accompanied by an ever-increasing dependency on natural gas in different parts of the planet. ●

Phantom Energy

Natural gas is a colorless, odorless fluid that contains between 70 and 90 percent methane, the component that makes it useful as a source of energy.

3 DISTRIBUTION
After being distilled and converted essentially into methane, natural gas is distributed for use through gas pipelines.

4 LIQUEFACTION
When it must be transported by sea or stored, the gas is compressed and cooled to -258° F (-161° C) to liquefy it.

2 REFINEMENT
The solid and wet components are separated. Then the byproducts, like propane and ethylene, are separated.

1 EXTRACTION
The gas is extracted from the deposit through a hole. When the gas is under pressure, it rises to the surface on its own. When it is not under pressure, it must be pumped.

LPG

Liquefied petroleum gas (LPG) is a byproduct of natural gas. It is bottled in cylinders and used by people who live in remote areas to operate, for instance, boilers and motors.

Deposit
Gas tends to be located inside porous rocks capped by impermeable rocks that are not necessarily associated with petroleum.

Lossless Trip

Among the many virtues of natural gas is the efficiency with which it can be transported. From gas deposits, it can be sent thousands of miles by ship or through gas pipelines with minimal losses.

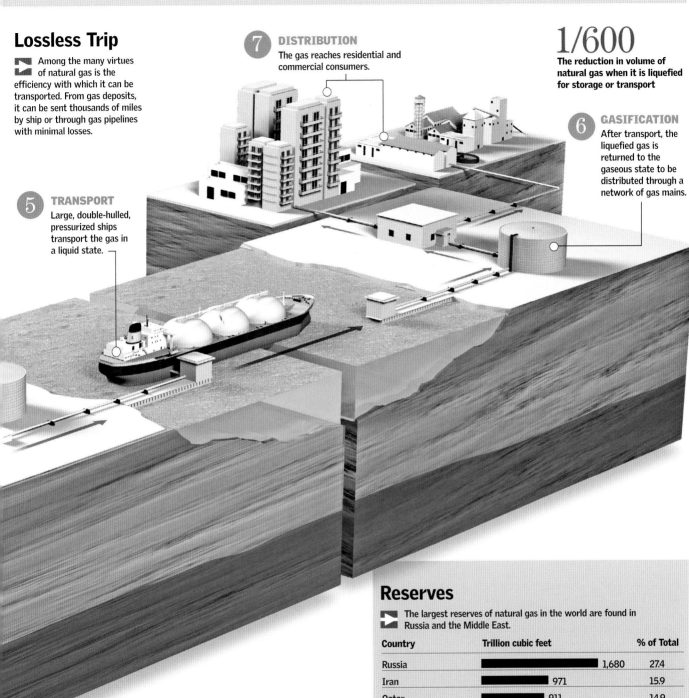

(7) DISTRIBUTION
The gas reaches residential and commercial consumers.

1/600

The reduction in volume of natural gas when it is liquefied for storage or transport

(6) GASIFICATION
After transport, the liquefied gas is returned to the gaseous state to be distributed through a network of gas mains.

(5) TRANSPORT
Large, double-hulled, pressurized ships transport the gas in a liquid state.

Dry gas deposits

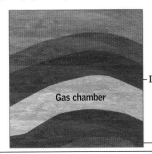

Gas chamber

Impermeable rock

Petroleum deposits

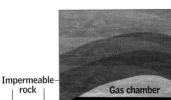

Gas chamber

Petroleum

Reserves

The largest reserves of natural gas in the world are found in Russia and the Middle East.

Country	Trillion cubic feet	% of Total
Russia	1,680	27.4
Iran	971	15.9
Qatar	911	14.9
Saudi Arabia	241	3.9
United Arab Emirates	214	3.5
United States	204	3.3
Nigeria	185	3.0
Algeria	161	2.6
Venezuela	151	2.5
Iraq	112	1.8
Indonesia	98	1.6
Norway	84	1.4
Malaysia	75	1.2
Rest of the world	1,037	16.9

6,124

trillion cubic feet is the total of the known reserves in the world.

Hydroelectric Energy

A bout 20 percent of the world's electricity is generated by the force of rivers through the use of hydroelectric power plants. This technology, used since the 19th century, employs a renewable, nonpolluting resource, although the technology's impact on the environment is high. According to the United Nations, two thirds of the world's hydroelectric potential is being used, especially in North America and Europe.

Diversion of the river

Charging chamber

Pipes

Powerhouse

River

Turbine Room

The place where the kinetic energy of the rivers is transformed into mechanical energy by turbines and later into electrical energy by generators

1 Water
enters the powerhouse under pressure and is injected into the turbine.

Needle
controls the pressure of the water injected into the wheels.

Generator
transforms the mechanical energy of the turbines into electrical energy.

Wheel
The force of the water on the blades makes it spin.

2 Turbine
The force of the water on its blades causes the turbine to turn.

Injectors
inject water under pressure onto the turbine wheel.

3 Energy
The turbine makes the generator turn, thereby producing electric energy. The water is returned to the river.

From the Dam to the City

Electricity generated by the power plant is sent to a transformer, where its voltage is increased for transmission.

The electrical energy circulates through high-voltage power grids over great distances.

A transformer lowers the voltage of the electricity before distributing it to homes.

Bypass Plant

1 Does not have a reservoir. It simply takes advantage of the available flow of water and thus is at the mercy of seasonal variations in water flow. It also cannot take advantage of occasional surplus water.

Plants with Reservoirs

2 The presence of a reservoir, formed by a containment dam, guarantees a constant flow of water—and, therefore, of energy—independent of variations in water level.

1 The water enters the powerhouse and turns the turbines. The generators produce electricity.

2 Once used, the water is returned to the river.

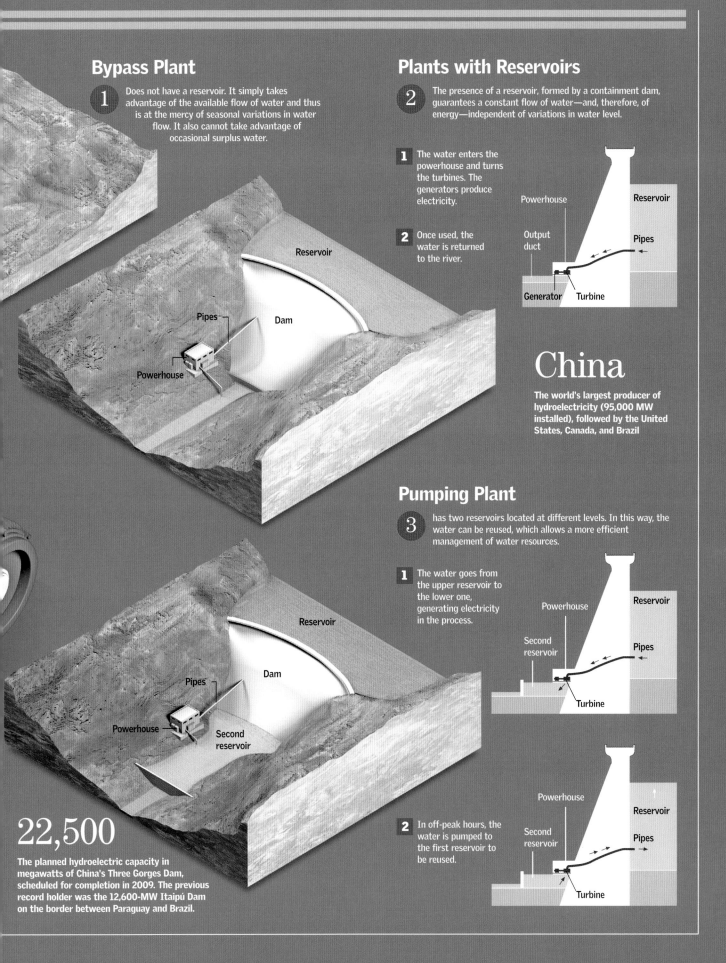

Reservoir

Dam

Pipes

Powerhouse

Powerhouse
Reservoir
Output duct
Pipes
Generator   Turbine

China

The world's largest producer of hydroelectricity (95,000 MW installed), followed by the United States, Canada, and Brazil

Pumping Plant

3 has two reservoirs located at different levels. In this way, the water can be reused, which allows a more efficient management of water resources.

1 The water goes from the upper reservoir to the lower one, generating electricity in the process.

Powerhouse
Reservoir
Second reservoir
Pipes
Turbine

2 In off-peak hours, the water is pumped to the first reservoir to be reused.

Powerhouse
Reservoir
Second reservoir
Pipes
Turbine

Reservoir

Dam

Pipes

Powerhouse

Second reservoir

22,500

The planned hydroelectric capacity in megawatts of China's Three Gorges Dam, scheduled for completion in 2009. The previous record holder was the 12,600-MW Itaipú Dam on the border between Paraguay and Brazil.

Nuclear Energy

One of the most efficient and cleanest methods for obtaining electric energy is through a controlled nuclear reaction. Although this technology has been used for half a century, it continues to be at the center of debate because of the risks it poses to the environment and health and because of the highly toxic waste it creates.

Fission

The nuclei of certain atoms, like uranium-235, can be broken apart when bombarded by neutrons. In doing so, they release great amounts of energy and new neutrons that can break down the nuclei of other atoms, generating a chain reaction.

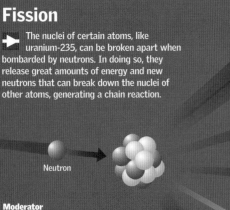

Neutron

Neutron

Neutron

Energy

Moderator
To achieve the breakdown of the nucleus, the neutrons must collide with it at a specific speed, which is governed by a moderating substance, such as water, heavy water, graphite, and so on.

Nucleus of a uranium-235 atom

Generation of Energy

The purpose of nuclear fission is to create very hot steam to operate turbines and electrical generators. The high temperatures are achieved by using nuclear energy from the reactor.

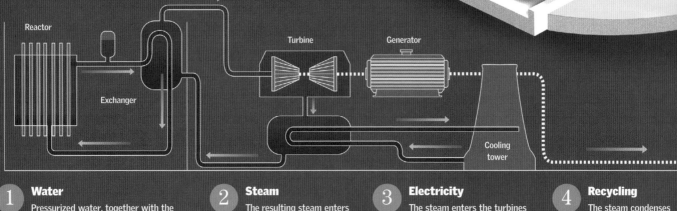

Reactor

Exchanger

Turbine

Generator

Cooling tower

1 Water
Pressurized water, together with the moderator, is pumped through the core of the reactor, and the temperature of the core increases by hundreds of degrees.

2 Steam
The resulting steam enters an exchanger, where it heats water until it too is converted into steam.

3 Electricity
The steam enters the turbines and makes them run. The turbines drive the generator that produces electricity.

4 Recycling
The steam condenses into liquid water and is reused.

370,000

Power, in megawatts (MW), generated by nuclear energy throughout the world

Uranium

In nature, uranium appears associated with other minerals. In addition, only 0.7 percent of uranium is the isotope uranium-235, necessary for nuclear fission. The proportion of uranium-235 must be increased 3 to 5 percent in a process called enrichment.

1 The original mineral is treated until a substance called yellowcake is obtained that is 80 percent uranium.

2 During conversion, first uranium tetrafluoride (UF4) and then uranium hexafluoride (UF6) are obtained.

3 The gaseous uranium hexafluoride is spun repeatedly in a centrifuge until it attains the desired concentration of uranium-235.

4 The enriched uranium gas is solidified again.

5 Through compaction, pellets of enriched uranium are obtained that can be used as fuel in nuclear reactors.

6 The pellets are put into hollow bars that are later placed in the core of the nuclear reactor.

UF4

UF4

Mobile crane
moves the mechanism that replenishes the reactor with nuclear fuel.

Reactor core
contains the radioactive fuel and is where the nuclear reaction takes place.

Separators
separate the liquid water from the steam.

Steam to the turbines

Hot water pipes

Cold water pipes

Pump
maintains the circulation of the fluids in the system.

Transformer

5 **Transport**
Before transmitting electricity, a transformer increases its voltage.

436

The number of nuclear plants operating throughout the world. More than 30 are in various stages of construction.

Fuel rod

Uranium pellets

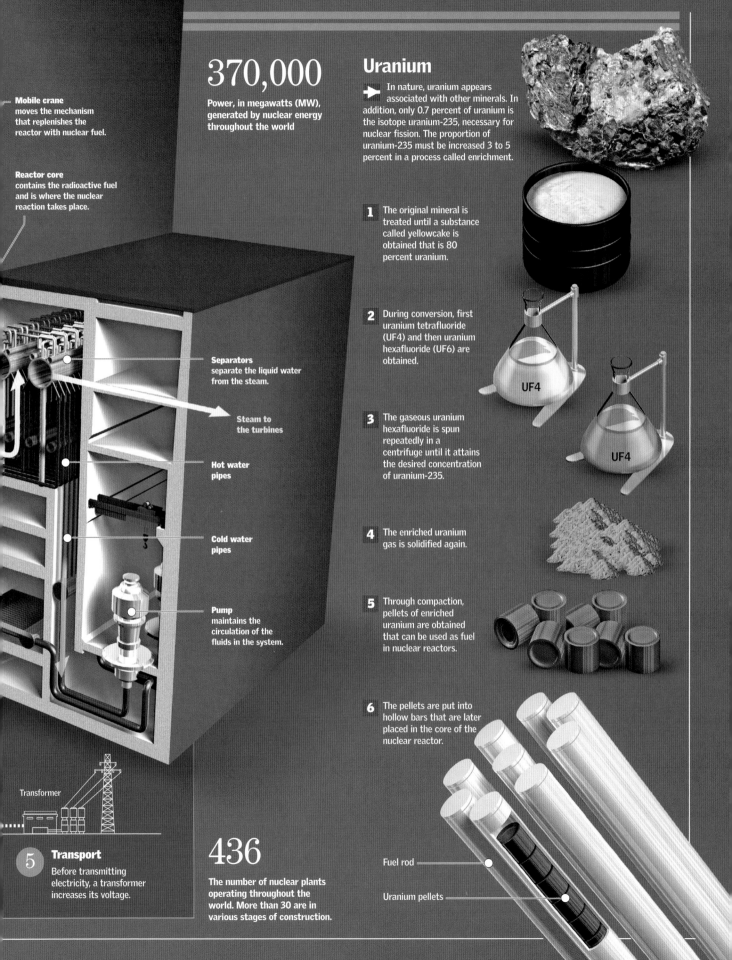

Solar Energy

The harnessing of solar energy to produce electricity and heat for everyday use is gaining popularity. Applications of this clean, unlimited form of energy range from charging batteries in telecommunications satellites, to public transportation, all the way to the solar households being built in greater numbers throughout the world.

ENERGY REGULATOR

Photovoltaic Energy

The energy obtained from sunlight. Requires the use of solar or photovoltaic cells.

SOLAR CELL

It is essentially formed by a thin layer of semiconductor material (silicon, for example), where the photovoltaic effect—the transformation of light into electrical energy—takes place.

1 The Sun shines on the cell. Some very energetic photons move the electrons and make them jump to the illuminated face of the cell.

Photon
Electron (-)

2 The negatively charged electrons generate a negative terminal on the illuminated face and leave an empty space in the positively charged dark face (positive terminal).

Electricity to the network

3 Once the circuit is closed, there is a constant flow of electrons (electric current) from the negative terminal to the positive one.

4 The current is maintained as long as the Sun illuminates the cell.

Upper metallic grid contact (negative electrode)

Upper metallic grid contact (positive electrode)

Negative contact (-)

Negative semiconductor (-) (mostly silicon)

Active charge carrier zone

Positive semiconductor (+) (mostly silicon)

Positive contact (+)

Investment

One of the main problems with using solar energy on an industrial scale is the high startup cost required to harness the energy; this cost keeps solar energy from competing with other cheaper energy sources.

Solar Heating

Another use of sunlight is as a source for heating water as well as for heating homes. In this case, solar collectors are used; unlike photovoltaic cells, the solar collectors do not produce electric energy.

180° F (82° C)

The maximum temperature a solar collector can reach when used to heat a house or to simply boil water

THE COLLECTOR

works using the greenhouse effect. It absorbs the heat from the Sun and then prevents this heat from being lost. In doing so, it warms a pipe, through which the fluid (water or gas) flows, that in turn heats a tank (exchanger).

Protective Cover

is formed by one or several glass plates. It lets sunlight through but retains the heat accumulated in the collector.

Absorption Plate

contains tubing, generally made of copper, through which the fluid heated in the collector flows.

Thermal Plate

The reflecting material and the black color absorb as much of the Sun's heat as possible. The protective plate then prevents any loss.

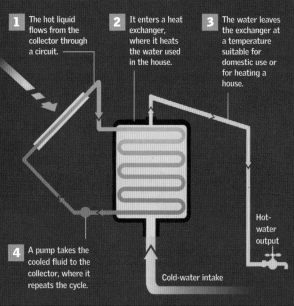

HOT WATER AND HEATING CIRCUIT

1 The hot liquid flows from the collector through a circuit.

2 It enters a heat exchanger, where it heats the water used in the house.

3 The water leaves the exchanger at a temperature suitable for domestic use or for heating a house.

4 A pump takes the cooled fluid to the collector, where it repeats the cycle.

Hot-water output

Cold-water intake

Other Applications

In almost every system powered by electricity, solar energy can play a central role without endangering the environment. Although this technology is presently more expensive to use than coal, natural gas, or petroleum, this difference in cost could change soon.

Space

Its use has extended to probes and satellites so that today hardly any spacecraft are designed without solar panels.

Transportation

The great challenge. Many prototypes of solar cars have been built, and some cities are already experimenting with buses.

Electronics

Calculators, watches, radios, flashlights, and so on. Almost any battery-powered device can be powered by solar energy.

Wind Energy

O ne of the most promising renewable energy resources is the use of wind to produce electricity by driving enormous wind turbines (windmills). Eolic power is an inexhaustible, clean, nonpolluting source of energy with more advantages than disadvantages. The most important disadvantages are our inability to predict precisely the force and direction of winds and the possibly negative impact that groups of large towers could have on the local landscape. ●

The Turbine

converts the wind into electrical energy through the use of simple technology based on mechanical gears.

Low-speed axle
turns slowly, between 20 to 35 revolutions per minute (rpm).

Multiplier
With gears, it multiplies by 50 the speed of rotation of the high-speed axle.

High-speed axle
turns at around 1,500 rpm, allowing it to operate the generator.

Generator
produces electric energy from the mechanical energy of the axle.

Computer
controls the conditions of the wind turbine and its orientation.

1 The wind
moves the blades of the wind turbine, producing mechanical energy, which is then converted into electrical energy.

Brakes
are activated when the winds surpass 74 miles per hour (120 km/h), preventing damage to the wind turbine.

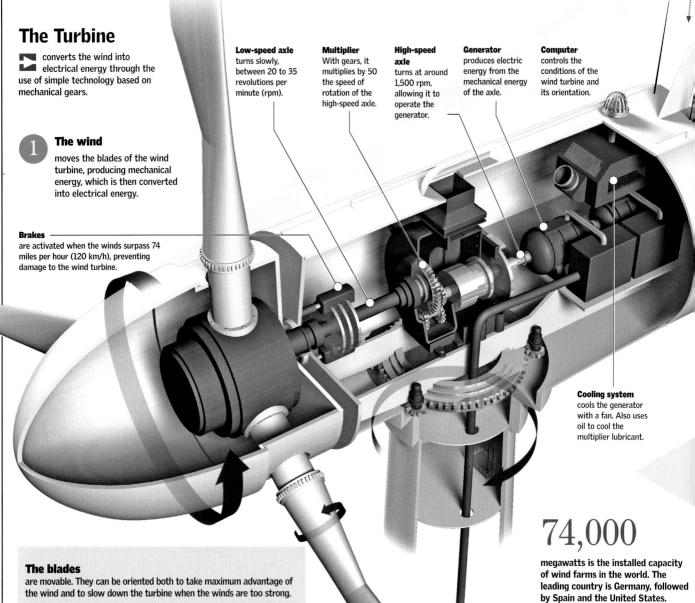

Cooling system
cools the generator with a fan. Also uses oil to cool the multiplier lubricant.

74,000
megawatts is the installed capacity of wind farms in the world. The leading country is Germany, followed by Spain and the United States.

The blades
are movable. They can be oriented both to take maximum advantage of the wind and to slow down the turbine when the winds are too strong.

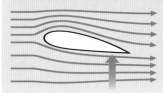

When facing the wind, their shape causes a pressure difference between the two faces of the wind turbine's blades. The pressure on the blades produces a force that turns the rotor.

2 Energy
The electric energy produced by the generator goes down the cables to a converter.

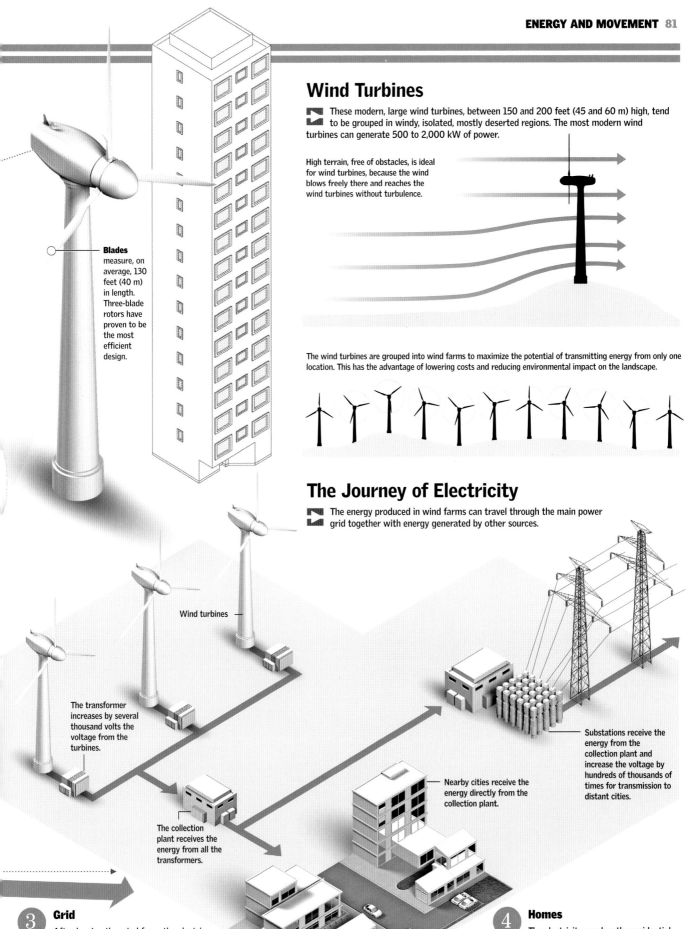

Wind Turbines

These modern, large wind turbines, between 150 and 200 feet (45 and 60 m) high, tend to be grouped in windy, isolated, mostly deserted regions. The most modern wind turbines can generate 500 to 2,000 kW of power.

High terrain, free of obstacles, is ideal for wind turbines, because the wind blows freely there and reaches the wind turbines without turbulence.

Blades
measure, on average, 130 feet (40 m) in length. Three-blade rotors have proven to be the most efficient design.

The wind turbines are grouped into wind farms to maximize the potential of transmitting energy from only one location. This has the advantage of lowering costs and reducing environmental impact on the landscape.

The Journey of Electricity

The energy produced in wind farms can travel through the main power grid together with energy generated by other sources.

Wind turbines

The transformer increases by several thousand volts the voltage from the turbines.

Substations receive the energy from the collection plant and increase the voltage by hundreds of thousands of times for transmission to distant cities.

Nearby cities receive the energy directly from the collection plant.

The collection plant receives the energy from all the transformers.

3 Grid
After leaving the wind farm, the electric energy can be incorporated into the main distribution grid.

4 Homes
The electricity reaches the residential distribution grid and finally homes.

Biofuels

asoline or diesel with added alcohol (ethanol) produced from crops such as corn appear more and more promising as solutions to the problems posed by the eventual exhaustion of the Earth's petroleum reserves, as well as the high cost of fossil fuels on the global market. However, this type of energy presents new challenges. One item of environmental concern is the possibility that massive exploitation of biofuels could lead to the replacement of jungles and woodlands with single-crop plantations meant only for the production of raw plant materials. ●

Ethanol

This is the alcohol in the medicine cabinets of our homes. It can be used in its pure form as a fuel or combined with gasoline in different proportions. The greater its purity, the greater are the engine modifications required to burn the fuel. Two common mixtures are E10 and E85, which have 10 percent and 85 percent ethanol, respectively.

1 HARVEST
Sugarcane, beets, corn, yucca, potatoes, and even wood can be used, with varying degrees of efficiency, to produce ethanol.

2 MILLING
The raw material is milled, and the resulting flour is mixed with water. Later an enzyme is added that helps convert starch into sugar.

3 COOKING
The mixture is cooked at 300° F (150° C) (sterilization) and is finally cooled with a water-refrigeration system.

4 FERMENTATION
Yeast is added to convert sugar into ethanol. This process, which produces heat and carbon dioxide, lasts 60 hours. When finished, the mixture, called mash, is 15 percent ethanol.

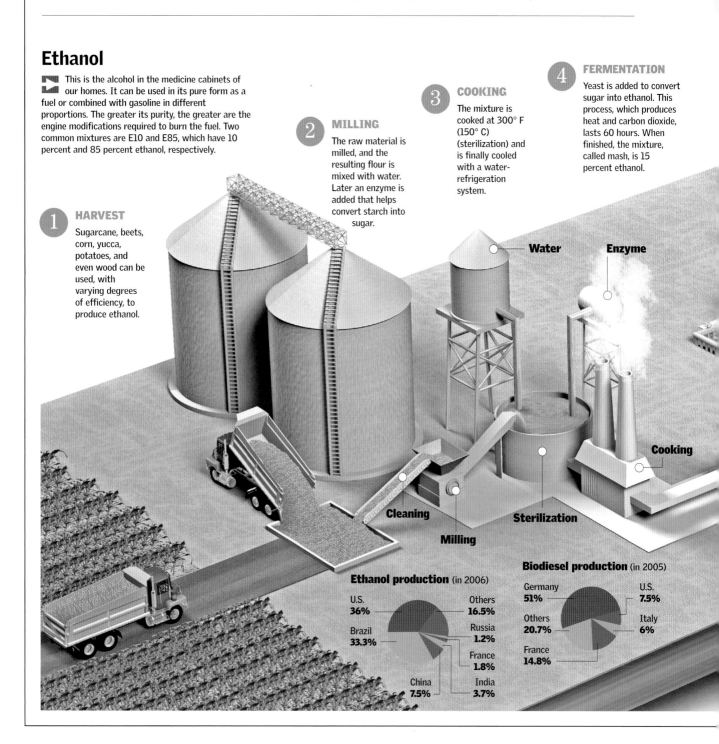

Water

Enzyme

Cooking

Cleaning

Milling

Sterilization

Ethanol production (in 2006)

U.S. **36%**
Brazil **33.3%**
China **7.5%**
Others **16.5%**
Russia **1.2%**
France **1.8%**
India **3.7%**

Biodiesel production (in 2005)

Germany **51%**
Others **20.7%**
France **14.8%**
U.S. **7.5%**
Italy **6%**

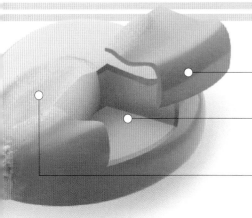

KERNEL OF CORN

HULL
protects the seed from water, insects, and microorganisms.

ENDOSPERM
represents 70 percent of the weight of the dry grain. It contains starch, the substance used to produce ethanol.

GERM
The most valuable and the only living part of the grain. In addition to containing the genetic material, vitamins, and minerals, it is 25 percent oil.

Byproducts

are generated during the production of ethanol. Anhydrous carbon is used in the manufacture of soft drinks. The stillage, a very nutritious residue, is used to feed cattle.

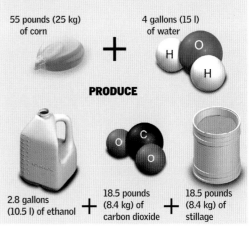

55 pounds (25 kg) of corn

$+$

4 gallons (15 l) of water

PRODUCE

2.8 gallons (10.5 l) of ethanol

$+$

18.5 pounds (8.4 kg) of carbon dioxide

$+$

18.5 pounds (8.4 kg) of stillage

5 **DISTILLATION**
The mixture is distilled first by evaporation to obtain 96 percent pure ethanol. It is later distilled by a molecular filtration process that can produce ethanol that is almost entirely pure. A 5 percent gasoline mixture is used for transportation.

6 **USE**
Ethanol is added to gasolines in different proportions to be used in vehicles. Gasolines with ethanol content between 10 and 30 percent do not require vehicle engines to have special modifications.

Yeast

Carbon dioxide collection

Gasoline

Fermentation tanks

Distillation

Refrigeration

70%
of the world's ethanol production is accounted for by Brazil and the United States. In Brazil, ethanol is made from sugarcane, and in the United States, it is made from corn.

Biodigesters

When anaerobic bacteria (bacteria that do not require oxygen to live) decompose organic material through processes such as rotting and fermentation, they release biogas that can be used as an energy resource for heating and for generating electricity. They also create mud with very high nutritional value, which can be used in agriculture or fish production. This technology appears promising as an energy alternative for rural and isolated regions, where, in addition to serving the energy needs of the populace, it helps recycle organic wastes.

The Reactor

is a closed chamber where the bacteria break down the waste. The generated gas (called biogas) and the fertilizing mud are collected for later use.

2 Digestion chamber
Where the bacteria ferment the waste. They produce gas and fertilizing mud.

3 Biogas
is a product of the process that contains methane and carbon dioxide. It is used for cooking, heating, and generating electricity.

4 Fertilizing mud
Very rich in nutrients and odorless, it is ideal for agricultural uses.

1 Waste
The organic wastes are introduced into the reactor and mixed with water.

Dome
is built underground and can be lined with concrete, brick, or stone.

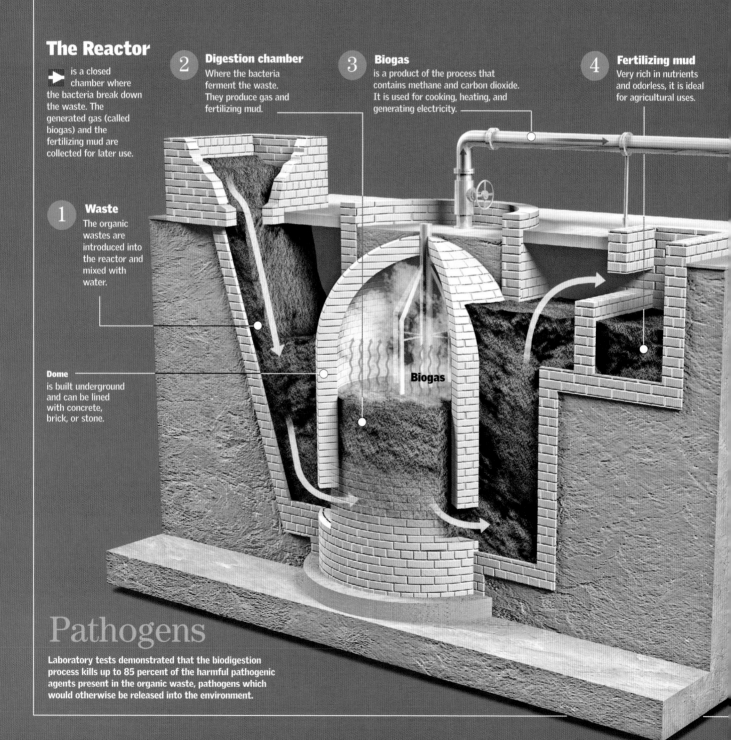

Biogas

Pathogens

Laboratory tests demonstrated that the biodigestion process kills up to 85 percent of the harmful pathogenic agents present in the organic waste, pathogens which would otherwise be released into the environment.

Ecological Cycle

Through recycling, biodigester technology offers an alternative to the problem of organic trash, with which more and more large cities and agro-industries must contend.

Fish-farming development

Organic Wastes

can be used both in urban and in rural regions.

Soil treatment

Exeter

In 1895, this English city was the first to inaugurate a public lighting system powered by biogas (from a water-purification plant).

FERTILIZING MUD

Biofertilizers

Gas for domestic use

BIOGAS

BIOGAS

Industrial Biogas Plant

produces great quantities of gas and fertilizer.

Generation of Electricity

Biogas can be used to produce electricity, although on a small scale.

Gas for automotive use

Electricity for domestic use

Biogas

The gaseous product of biodigestion, it is made up of a mixture of gases whose makeup depends on the composition of the wastes and the break-down process.

55-70%	30-45%	1-10%	0.5-3%	0.1%
Methane (CH$_4$)	**Carbon Dioxide (CO$_2$)**	**Hydrogen (H$_2$)**	**Nitrogen (N$_2$)**	**Sulfuric Acid (H$_2$S)**
The energy-producing component of biogas	A greenhouse gas. It must be removed from biogas for certain uses.	Gas present in the atmosphere	Gas present in the atmosphere	Corrosive and highly polluting agent. It has to be removed.

Equivalencies

The energy potential contained in one pound of gasoline can be obtained from three pounds of organic wastes.

Geothermal Energy

I s one of the cleanest and most promising sources of energy. The first geothermal plant started operating more than 100 years ago. Geothermal plants generate electricity from the heat that emanates from the Earth's interior. Geothermal power plants, however, suffer from some limitations, such as the fact that they must be constructed in regions with high volcanic activity. The possibility of this kind of plant becoming defunct due to a reduction in such volcanic activity is always present. ●

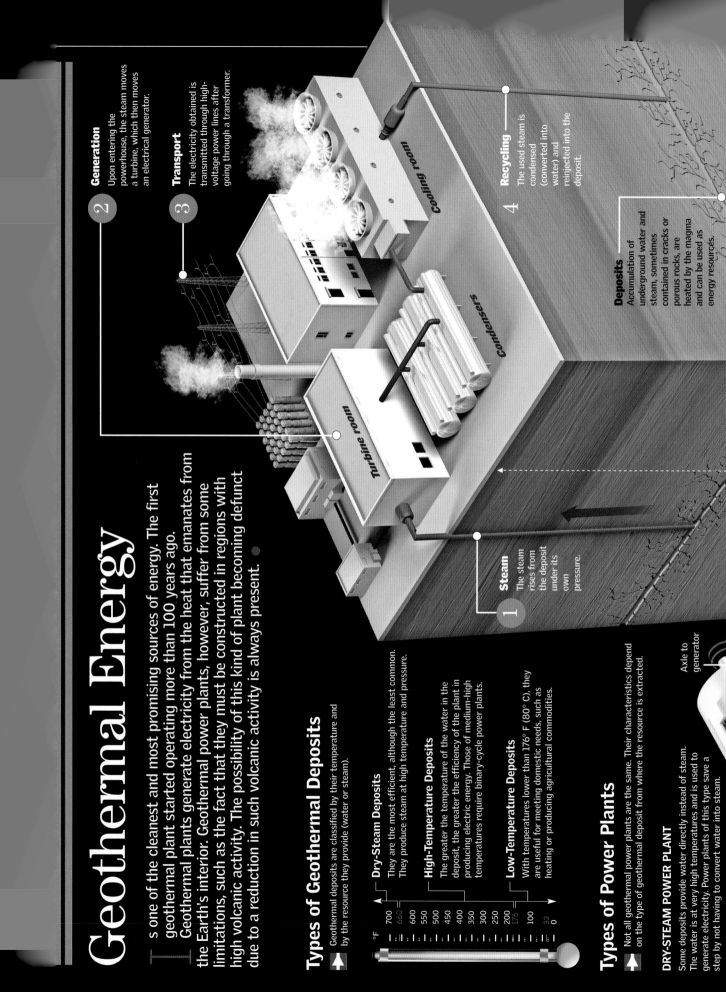

2 Generation
Upon entering the powerhouse, the steam moves a turbine, which then moves an electrical generator.

3 Transport
The electricity obtained is transmitted through high-voltage power lines after going through a transformer.

4 Recycling
The used steam is condensed (converted into water) and reinjected into the deposit.

Cooling room

Condensers

Turbine room

Deposits
Accumulation of underground water and steam, sometimes contained in cracks or porous rocks, are heated by the magma and can be used as energy resources.

1 Steam
The steam rises from the deposit under its own pressure.

Types of Geothermal Deposits

Geothermal deposits are classified by their temperature and by the resource they provide (water or steam).

°F
700
660
600
550
500
450
400
350
300
250
200
176
100
32
0

Dry-Steam Deposits
They are the most efficient, although the least common. They produce steam at high temperature and pressure.

High-Temperature Deposits
The greater the temperature of the water in the deposit, the greater the efficiency of the plant in producing electric energy. Those of medium-high temperatures require binary-cycle power plants.

Low-Temperature Deposits
With temperatures lower than 176° F (80° C), they are useful for meeting domestic needs, such as heating or producing agricultural commodities.

Types of Power Plants

Not all geothermal power plants are the same. Their characteristics depend on the type of geothermal deposit from where the resource is extracted.

DRY-STEAM POWER PLANT
Some deposits provide water directly instead of steam. The water is at very high temperatures and is used to generate electricity. Power plants of this type save a step by not having to convert water into steam.

Axle to generator

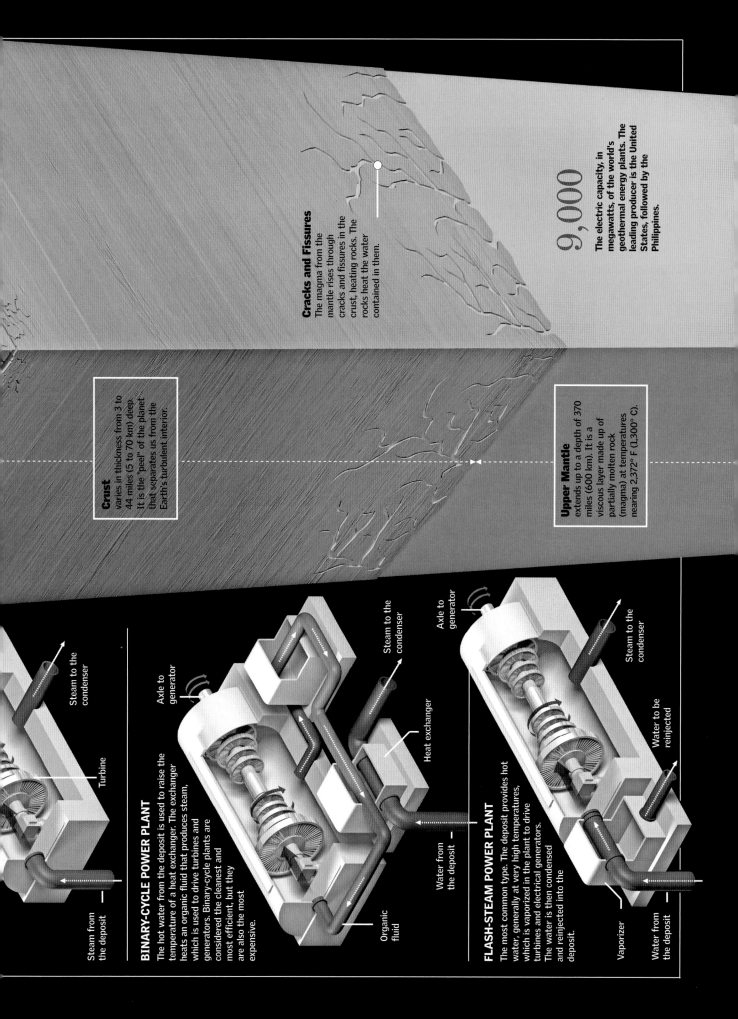

Cracks and Fissures
The magma from the mantle rises through cracks and fissures in the crust, heating rocks. The rocks heat the water contained in them.

Crust
varies in thickness from 3 to 44 miles (5 to 70 km) deep. It is the "peel" of the planet that separates us from the Earth's turbulent interior.

Upper Mantle
extends up to a depth of 370 miles (600 km). It is a viscous layer made up of partially molten rock (magma) at temperatures nearing 2,372° F (1,300° C).

9,000
The electric capacity, in megawatts, of the world's geothermal energy plants. The leading producer is the United States, followed by the Philippines.

Steam to the condenser

Turbine

Steam from the deposit

BINARY-CYCLE POWER PLANT
The hot water from the deposit is used to raise the temperature of a heat exchanger. The exchanger heats an organic fluid that produces steam, which is used to drive turbines and generators. Binary-cycle plants are considered the cleanest and most efficient, but they are also the most expensive.

Axle to generator

Steam to the condenser

Heat exchanger

Water from the deposit

Organic fluid

FLASH-STEAM POWER PLANT
The most common type. The deposit provides hot water, generally at very high temperatures, which is vaporized in the plant to drive turbines and electrical generators. The water is then condensed and reinjected into the deposit.

Axle to generator

Steam to the condenser

Water to be reinjected

Vaporizer

Water from the deposit

Tidal Energy

The variations in the tides and the force of the oceans' waves signify an enormous energy potential for generating electricity without emitting polluting gases into the atmosphere or depleting resources, as happens in the case of fossil fuels. Tidal plants are similar to hydroelectric plants. They have a water-retention dam (which crosses an estuary from shore to shore) and a powerhouse where the turbines and generators to produce electricity are located. ●

Gates
are opened to let the water in as the tide rises and then closed to prevent its exit.

The Tides

Responding to the Moon's gravitational pull on the Earth, the oceans' tides rise and fall twice a day.

High Tide
The Moon attracts the waters of the sea, and the tide rises.

Amplitude of the Tides
To produce electricity efficiently, the variance between high and low tide needs to be at least 13 feet (4 m); this variation limits the number of possible locations for tidal plants.

Low Tide
When the Moon is to one side of the Earth, the water recedes.

Gates
regulate the exit of trapped water, through the turbines, during the generation of electricity.

Turbines
are powered by the flow of the water. Upon turning, they move the generators that produce electricity.

Foundations
are built from concrete to prevent the erosion produced by the flow of water over the terrain.

12 hours 25 minutes

The approximate time between two high tides or low tides, depending on the geographic location and sometimes on other factors, such as winds and ocean currents

Tidal Power Plant

The turbines, which power the generators, are found inside the plant. They convert the kinetic energy of the water into mechanical energy and then into electrical energy.

Dam

crosses the estuary or bay from shore to shore. It retains the water during high tide.

Location of the Dam

The power plant needs be located in a river outlet to the sea (estuary) or in a narrow bay—places that have above-average tidal amplitude (the variance between low tide and high tide).

Sea

Dam

Estuary

Electrical Substation

increases the voltage of the generated power before its transmission.

High-Voltage Grid

takes the electrical energy to the regions where it will be consumed.

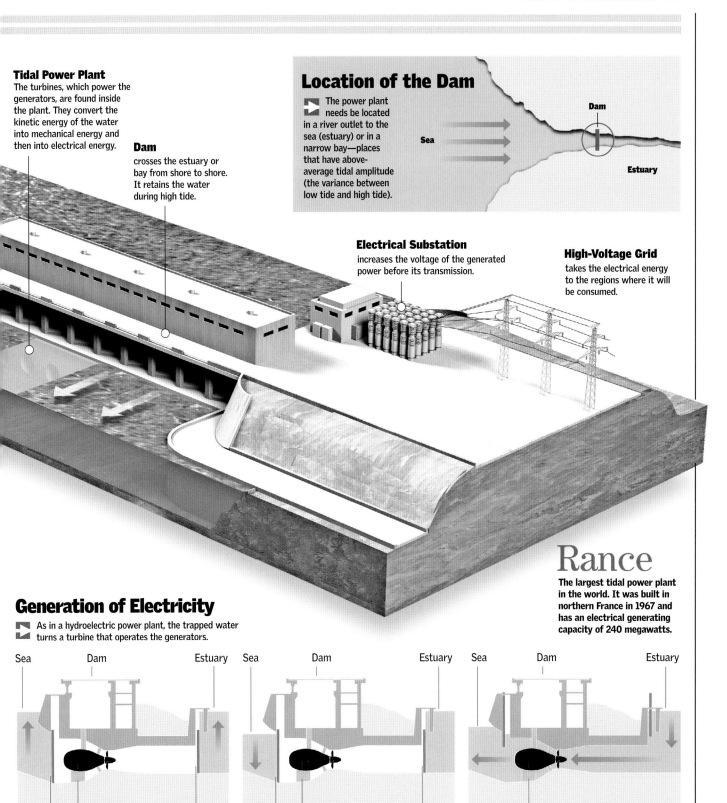

Rance

The largest tidal power plant in the world. It was built in northern France in 1967 and has an electrical generating capacity of 240 megawatts.

Generation of Electricity

As in a hydroelectric power plant, the trapped water turns a turbine that operates the generators.

Sea | Dam | Estuary
Gate | Turbine | Gate

Sea | Dam | Estuary
Gate | Turbine | Gate

Sea | Dam | Estuary
Turbine

1 High Tide
During high tide, the level of the water rises in the estuary. The gates of the dam are opened to let the water in.

2 Water Reservoir
Once high tide is complete, the water level in the estuary begins to drop. The gates of the dam are closed to prevent the trapped water from escaping.

3 Generation
During low tide, the trapped water is released and it passes through the system of turbines that power the electrical generators.

Hydrogen

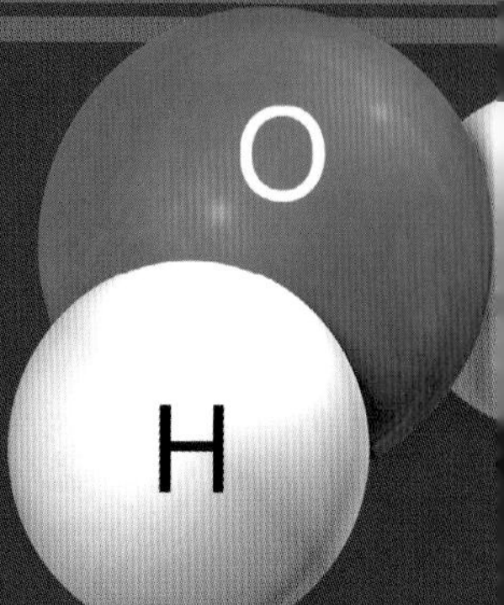

Some people consider hydrogen the energy source of the future and predict that in the short term it will gain widespread use in place of fossil fuels. The hydrogen is combined with oxygen to release energy to generate electricity. Among the advantages of hydrogen-based energy are its very low pollution level (the byproduct of the reaction is water vapor) and its inexhaustibility (it can be recycled and reused). Disadvantages include the complications inherent in handling pure hydrogen, its costs, and the wide-scale conversion that would be necessary for petroleum-fueled engines and systems.

O

H

Fuel Cells

produce electricity from the energy released during the chemical reaction of hydrogen and oxygen. The engine converts the electrical energy into mechanical energy.

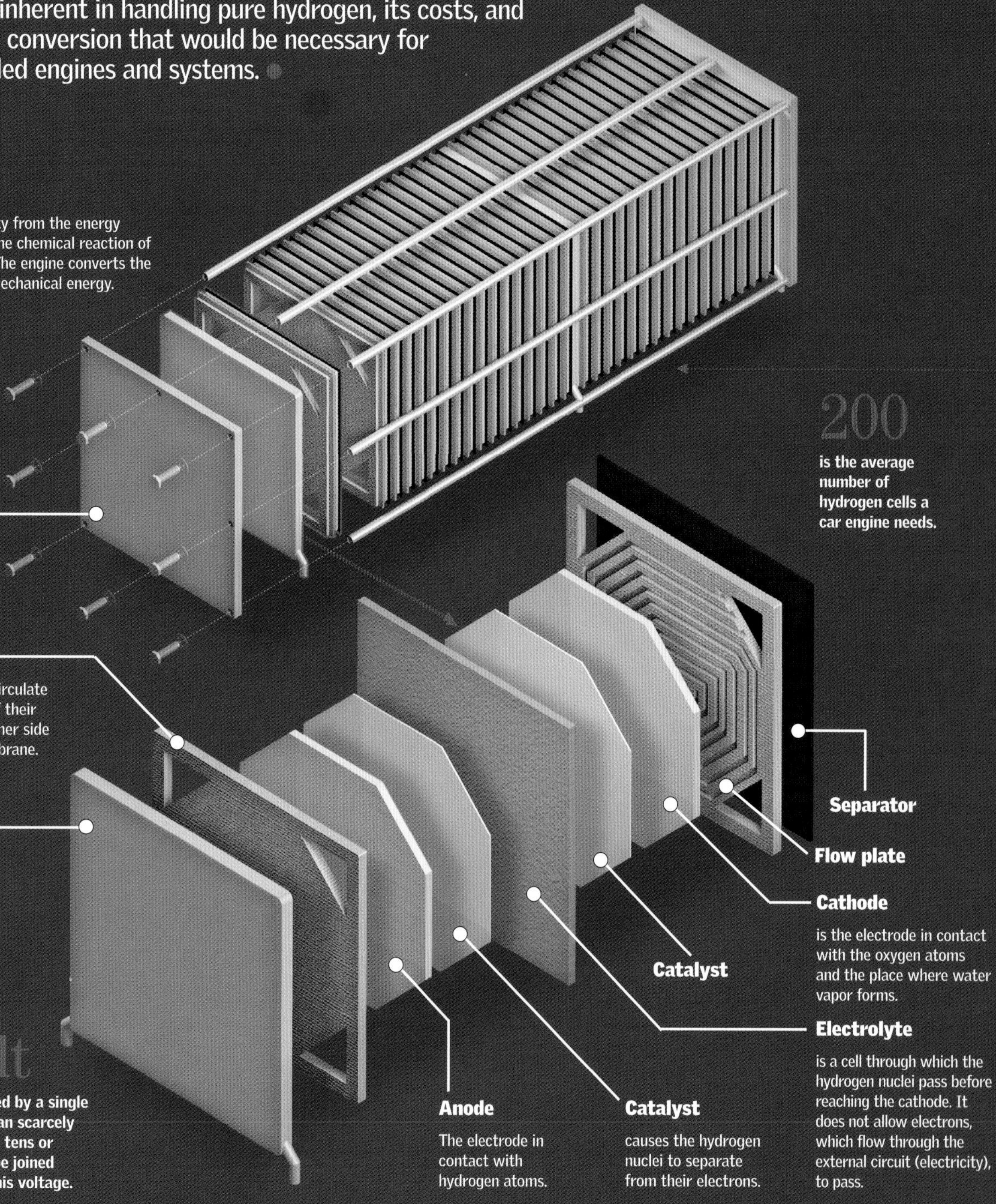

Fuel-cell pack

200

is the average number of hydrogen cells a car engine needs.

Flow plate

Hydrogen and oxygen circulate through the channels of their respective plates on either side of the electrolytic membrane.

Cooling cell

The cooling cell should be refrigerated because the reaction produced in the cell generates heat.

Separator

Flow plate

Cathode

is the electrode in contact with the oxygen atoms and the place where water vapor forms.

Catalyst

Electrolyte

is a cell through which the hydrogen nuclei pass before reaching the cathode. It does not allow electrons, which flow through the external circuit (electricity), to pass.

0.7 volt

is the voltage generated by a single fuel cell. This energy can scarcely light one lightbulb, but tens or hundreds of cells can be joined together to increase this voltage.

Anode

The electrode in contact with hydrogen atoms.

Catalyst

causes the hydrogen nuclei to separate from their electrons.

The Cleanest Car

➡ The latest hydrogen-fueled models can travel up to 100 miles per hour (160 km/h) and have a range between 170 and 250 miles (270 and 400 km), depending on whether liquid or compressed hydrogen is used.

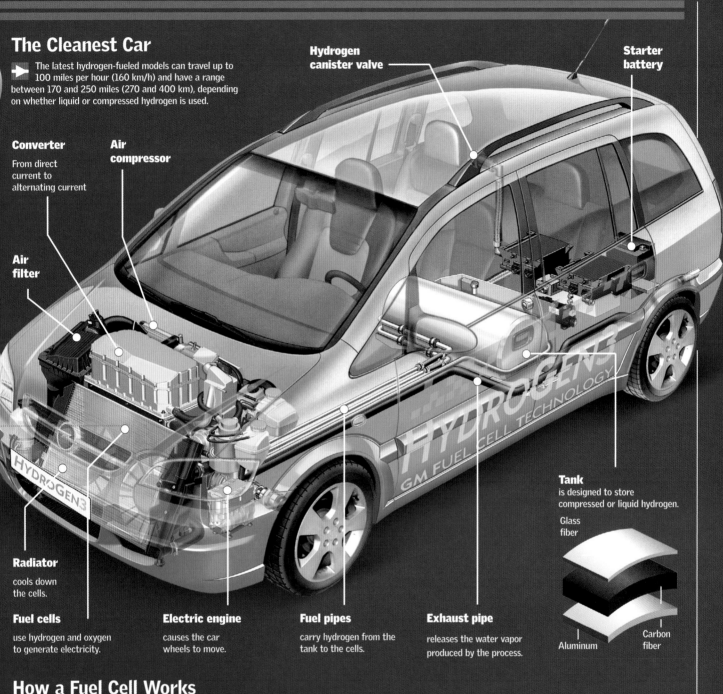

Hydrogen canister valve

Starter battery

Converter
From direct current to alternating current

Air compressor

Air filter

Radiator
cools down the cells.

Fuel cells
use hydrogen and oxygen to generate electricity.

Electric engine
causes the car wheels to move.

Fuel pipes
carry hydrogen from the tank to the cells.

Exhaust pipe
releases the water vapor produced by the process.

Tank
is designed to store compressed or liquid hydrogen.

Glass fiber

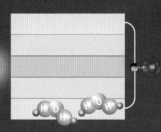

Aluminum

Carbon fiber

How a Fuel Cell Works

➡ The fuel cell produces electricity from the energy released when oxygen and hydrogen join to form water.

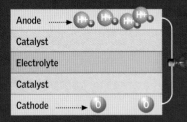

Anode
Catalyst
Electrolyte
Catalyst
Cathode

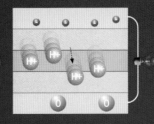

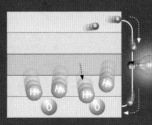

1 Hydrogen collects at the anode and oxygen at the cathode. The catalyst separates the hydrogen electrons from their nuclei.

2 Hydrogen nuclei cross the electrolytic layer without their electrons.

3 Electrons, which cannot cross the electrolytic layer, flow through the circuit until they reach the cathode, thereby producing electric current.

4 The byproducts of the process are water and heat. The reaction continues as long as fuel is supplied.

Glossary

Acid

An acid is any chemical compound that, when dissolved in water, produces a solution with a pH lower than 7.

Aerodynamics

Branch of fluid mechanics that studies interactions between a solid object and a surrounding fluid when there is a relative motion between them. To solve an aerodynamics problem, it is normally necessary to calculate various properties of the fluid, such as velocity, pressure, density, and temperature, as a function of the position of the object through time.

Air Balloon

Flying device that has a compartment for passengers and a bag of lightweight, impermeable material. This envelope assumes a more or less spherical shape when it is filled with a gas of lower density than air to produce a lift force greater than the balloon's weight.

Alkali

Name given to low density, colored, soft metals that react easily with halogens to form ionic salts and with water to form strongly basic hydroxides. They all have only one electron in their valence shell, which they tend to lose, forming singly charged ions.

Allotropy

Property of certain chemical elements appearing with different molecular structures, such as oxygen, which can appear as molecular oxygen (O_2) or ozone (O_3). Other examples are phosphorous, which can appear as red phosphorous or white phosphorous (P_4), and carbon, which can appear as graphite or diamond. For an element to be called an allotrope, its different molecular structures must be present in the same physical state.

Alternator

Machine that transforms mechanical energy into electric energy by using induction to generate an alternating current. Alternators are based on the principle that an electric voltage is induced in a conductor subjected to a variable magnetic field. The voltage's polarity depends on the direction of the field and on the magnitude of the flux that passes through the conductor. An alternator is made up of two fundamental parts: the inductor, which creates the magnetic field, and the conductor, which passes through the lines of force of the field.

Ampere

Unit of electric current. It is one of the basic units in the International System of Units. It is the current that, when flowing through two straight, parallel conductors of infinite length and of negligible circular cross-section and placed at a distance of 1 meter apart in a vacuum, produces a force of 2×10^{-7} newtons per meter of length. It is represented by the symbol A.

Anode

Name given to the positive electrode of an electrolytic cell toward which the negative ions move inside an electrolyte. For this reason, these ions are called anions. In the case of vacuum tubes, power supplies, batteries, and so forth, the anode is the electrode or terminal with higher potential.

Atomic Bomb

Bomb whose great destructive power is the result of the release of large amounts of energy in the fission (splitting) of atoms..

Baryon

A baryon is a hadron made up of three quarks that are bound by a strong nuclear interaction. The proton and neutron belong to this group.

Base

Substance that, when in aqueous solution, donates OH- ions to the medium. The generalized concept of pH is used for both acids and bases.

Biogas

Gaseous byproduct of biodigestion. It is composed of a mixture of gases, the proportions of which depend on the composition of the wastes and the product of the digestion.

Bit

Information in computers is stored in binary digits (bits).

Bond

Union between the atoms that form a compound or the force that holds together two chemical entities.

Catalyst

A substance that can accelerate or slow down a chemical reaction and is not consumed during the reaction.

Cathode

Name given to the negative electrode of an electrolytic cell toward which the positive ions, or cations, in an electrolyte move.

Coal

Organic mineral, black in color and combustible. It typically occurs under a layer of slate and over a layer of sand. It is believed that most coal was formed during the Carboniferous Period (299 to 359 million years ago).

Coil

Ensemble of a variable number of windings of a conductor, typically around a cylindrical core.

Convection

Convection is one of the three forms of heat transfer and is characterized by the displacement of matter between regions at different temperatures. Convection is produced only in fluids. When a fluid is heated, it becomes less dense and rises. As it rises, it is displaced by lower-temperature fluid that, in turn, is heated, thus repeating the cycle.

Coulomb

Amount of charge that a current of 1 ampere transmits in 1 second. A coulomb is equal to 6.28×10^{18} times the charge of an electron.

Dynamics

In physics, name given to the branch of mechanics that studies the motion of bodies subjected to the action of forces.

Dynamo

Direct-current generator that transforms mechanical energy into electric energy.

Electric Conductor

A body is an electric conductor if, when placed in contact with an electrically charged body, it transmits this electricity to all points of its surface.

Electric Motor

Transforms electric energy into mechanical energy. It can be powered by direct or alternating current.

Electricity

Phenomenon produced by positively or negatively charged particles, at rest or in motion. It is also the branch of physics that studies electric phenomena.

Electrolytic Cell

Device used to decompose ionized substances, called electrolytes, by means of an electric current. Electrolytes can be acids, bases, or salts. The process of dissociation or decomposition that takes place in an electrolytic cell is called electrolysis.

Fuse

Easy-to-melt metal wire or strip that is placed in electric installations, which melts to interrupt excessive current flow.

Fusibility

Property of many bodies to change from solid to liquid through the application of heat.

Gamma Rays

Electromagnetic radiation generated by radioactive elements, by subatomic processes (such as annihilation of an electron-positron pair), or in astrophysical phenomena of great violence. Because of their high energy, gamma rays are a type of ionizing radiation. They can penetrate matter very deeply and can produce severe damage to the nucleus of cells.

Gears

Ensemble of toothed wheels that mesh together or with a chain to transmit rotational motion from one driveshaft to another. The most common types are cylindrical, chain, conical, helical, worm, and rack-and-pinion.

Generator

Machine that produces electric energy from mechanical energy.

Geothermal Energy

Energy released by hot water or steam rising from underground, as in geysers.

Gravitation

Force of mutual attraction that is experienced by two objects with mass. It is one of the four fundamental forces known in nature. The effect of gravitation on a body tends to be associated, in common terms, with the concept of weight.

Helium

Chemical element with atomic number 2 and symbol He. It has the properties of a noble gas: it is inert (not chemically reactive), monoatomic, odorless, and colorless. Helium has the lowest evaporation point of all chemical elements and can be solidified only under very great pressure. In some natural gas deposits, it is found in large enough quantities for exploitation. It is used for filling balloons and blimps, as a liquid refrigerant for cryogenic superconducting materials, and in breathing-gas mixtures for deep-sea diving.

Hertz

Unit used to measure frequencies. A hertz is equivalent to a full cycle of one wave in 1 second.

Hydraulic Energy

Potential energy of water held by lakes or reservoirs.

Hydraulic Motor

Motor that produces mechanical energy from the energy present in a liquid.

Hydraulic Pump

Device that takes advantage of the kinetic energy of water to move part of the liquid to a higher level. There are two types: piston or centrifugal.

Hydraulic Turbine

Turbine that uses the energy of moving water.

Hydrogen

Chemical element with atomic number 1 and symbol H. At room temperature, it is a colorless, odorless, and flammable gas. Hydrogen is the lightest and most abundant chemical element in the universe. Most stars consist of this element in a plasma state during most of their life cycle. Additionally, it is present in many substances, including water and organic compounds, and is capable of reacting with most elements.

Hydrophone

Electric sound transducer that is used in water or other liquids, in a manner analogous to the use of a microphone in air. A hydrophone can also be used as an emitter, but not all hydrophones are capable of this. Hydrophones are used by geologists and geophysicists to detect seismic activity.

Induction

Phenomenon that gives rise to an electromotive force (voltage) in a medium or body exposed to a variable magnetic field or in a moving medium relative to a static magnetic field. If the body is a conductor, then an induced current is produced. This phenomenon was described by Michael Faraday, who expressed it indicating that the magnitude of the induced voltage is proportional to the variation of the magnetic field.

Isotope

The word *isotope* comes from Greek and means "at the same place," because all isotopes of an element are classified in the same place in the periodic table. Isotopes are denoted by the name of the element followed by the mass number, commonly separated by a hyphen (e.g., carbon-14, uranium-238, etc.). If the relationship between the number of protons and neutrons is not conducive to nuclear stability, then the isotope is radioactive.

Joule

Unit of energy and work that is defined as the work expended by a force of 1 newton over a displacement of 1 meter. It is also equal to 1 watt second, which electrically is the work done in 1 second by a potential difference of 1 volt with a current of 1 ampere.

Kinetic Energy

Energy of bodies when they are in motion.

Lever

One of the simplest machines. It consists of a bar that, when combined with a fulcrum, magnifies a force and makes it possible to lift a load with a relatively small effort.

Magnetic Declination

Name given to the difference, measured in degrees, that exists between the geographic North Pole and the magnetic North Pole.

Mass

Commonly defined as the amount of matter present in an object.

Metamaterials

Materials that, by being treated and shaped at the nanoscale level, acquire properties that do not exist in nature.

Nanotube

A hollow cylindrical tube, some 2 nanometers thick, made of carbon atoms.

Natural Gas

Gas with high heat content, composed of light hydrocarbons such as methane, ethane, propane, and butane.

Neutron

Heavy subatomic particle, with no electric charge and a mass approximately equal to that of the proton.

Newton

Unit of force that is defined as the force necessary to accelerate a 1 kg object by 1 m/s^2. Because weight is the force exerted by gravity on Earth, the newton is also a unit of weight. A mass of 1 kg has a weight of 9.81 N.

Nitroglycerin

A powerful, unstable explosive that is oily, odorless, and heavier than water. When combined with an absorbent body, it is known as dynamite. In medicine nitroglycerin is used as a vasodilator for the treatment of coronary ischemia, acute myocardial infarction, and congestive heart failure. It is administered transdermally, sublingually, or intravenously.

Nuclear Energy

Energy produced from nuclear reactions, such as the fission of uranium or plutonium atoms.

Nuclear Fission

Fission occurs when the atomic nucleus is divided into two or more smaller nuclei; it generates several other products, such as free neutrons and photons. This process results in the emission of large quantities of energy, generally in the form of gamma rays. Fission can be induced through several methods, including bombarding the nucleus of a fissionable atom with another particle of appropriate energy—generally a free neutron. This particle is absorbed by the nucleus, making it unstable. The process generates much more energy than would be released in a chemical reaction. This energy is emitted as gamma rays and as the kinetic energy of the resulting nuclei and neutrons.

Plasma

A gas at high temperature in which the atoms have broken apart, with the electrons separated from the atomic nuclei.

Polymers

Long chains of hundreds of thousands of smaller molecules that are joined through a process called polymerization.

Polyurethane

Polyurethane is a plastic material used in the formation of many high-performance synthetic paints (such as car paints and floor stains), foams, and elastic materials. It is a product that, in combustion, generates hydrocyanic compounds that are very dangerous to humans.

Propane

Propane is an odorless, colorless gas. It is an aliphatic hydrocarbon (alkene). Its chemical formula is C_3H_8. The main use of propane is as a fuel. In the chemical industry, it is one of the starting products in the synthesis of propylene. It is also used as a refrigerant gas and as an aerosol propellant.

Propulsion

Motion given to a body when a force acts on it. Also, the displacement of a body in a fluid, especially in the cases of self-propulsion in space.

Proton

Subatomic particle with a positive electric charge of 1 and a mass 1,836 times that of an electron. Some theories of particle physics predict that protons can decay despite being very stable, with a lower limit to their half-life of some 10^{35} years. The proton and the neutron together are known as nucleons because they form the nucleus of atoms.

Refraction

Deflection of a ray of light caused by changes in the speed of light as it passes from one medium to another.

Resistivity

Resistance that opposes the flow of electric current in a conductor at a given temperature. It is the inverse of conductivity.

Solar Cell

Photovoltaic cell that produces electric energy from solar radiation.

Solar Energy

Energy obtained by transforming the Sun's radiant energy into electric energy through the use of photovoltaic cells.

Thermodynamics

Branch of physics that studies energy, how it is transformed into its many manifestations (such as heat), and its capacity to do work. It is intimately related to statistical mechanics, from which many thermodynamic relationships can be derived. Thermodynamics studies physical systems at a macroscopic level, whereas statistical mechanics tends to describe them at the microscopic level.

Thermohaline Circulation

In physical oceanography, the name given to the convective circulation that globally affects the oceanic water masses. It is very important for its role in the net flow of heat from the tropics toward the poles.

Turbine

Machine that transforms the energy in the flow of fluid into mechanical energy or electric energy.

Vacuum Pump

Compressor used to extract air and uncondensed gases from a space, thereby reducing its pressure to below atmospheric pressure.

Vibrational Motion

Periodic, oscillatory motion in which an object moves about a point of equilibrium.

Volt

The potential difference along the length of a conductor when a 1 ampere current uses 1 watt of power. It can also be defined as the potential difference that exists between two points such that 1 joule of work is needed to move a charge of 1 coulomb from one point to the other.

Watt

Unit of power that is equivalent to 1 joule per second. Expressed in electric units, it is the power produced by a potential difference of 1 volt and an electric current of 1 ampere.

Wave Motion

Motion in which the perturbation of one point in a medium is propagated to distant points in the medium with a net transport of energy but not of matter.

Wind Energy

Energy obtained by converting the kinetic energy of the wind into mechanical energy through the rotation of an axle to operate a machine or electric generator.

Index

A

absolute motionless state, 58
absolute zero (temperature), 8, 9, 45, 51
AC (alternating current), 51, 53
acceleration, 30, 32, 33, 36
acid, 22-23
actinide element, 15
aerogel, 4, 27
alcohol: *See* ethanol
Algeria, natural gas reserves, 73
alkaline earth metal, 14
alkaline metal, 14
alloy, 18, 19
alpha (α) radiation, 24
alternating current (AC), 51, 53
alternative energy source, 67
ampere, 51
amplitude, 54, 88, 89
anaerobic bacteria, biodigestion, 84
anhydrous carbon, 83
antimatter, 9
Archimedes, 39
astronaut
    gravitational effects on, 10
    pressurized suits, 35
atmospheric pressure, 35
atom, 4, 6, 8, 12-13, 14, 15, 62
atomic bomb, 25, 26, 65
atomic nucleus, 12, 13, 24, 25, 31
atomic number, 12, 14
aurora borealis, 10, 47
automobile
    clean car, 90
    energy efficiency ratio, 43
    hydrogen-fueled, 90, 91
    solar energy use, 79
axle (wheels), 39

B

Baekeland, Leo, 20
Bakelite, 20
balloon, 34, 35, 44
base, 22, 23
base metal element, 15
bat (mammal), 54, 55
battery, 22, 43, 50, 78
bed of nails, fakir's secret, 34, 35
Bessemer, Henry, 19
beta (ß) radiation, 24
bicycle, 38-39, 43
binary-cycle power plant, 86, 87
binary system, 64
biodiesel, producers, 82
biodigestion, 68, 84-85
biofuel, 68, 82-83
biogas, 84
bit, 64, 65
black hole, 33
black light, 57
blackout, electrical, 48
bobsled (kinetic energy), 42-43
boiling point, 11, 35, 45
Bose-Einstein condensate, 9
Brazil
    ethanol production, 68, 82, 83
    hydroelectric production, 75
Britain: *See* United Kingdom
buffer solution, 23
butane, 71
bypass plant (hydroelectric energy), 75

C

calorie, 44, 45
Canada
    crude oil reserves, 71
    hydroelectric production, 75
car: *See* automobile

carbon fiber, 4, 26
catalyst, 17, 27
catalytic separation unit (petroleum
    production), 71
Celsius, Anders, 10
Celsius temperature scale, 10, 45
centrifugal force, 36
centripetal force, 36
chain reaction, 16, 25, 76
chemical effect, electricity, 49
chemical equation, 17
chemical reaction, 16-17
    catalyst, 17
    heat produced by, 44
    language of, 17
    law of conservation of matter, 17
    lighting a match, 16, 36
    types of, 17
China
    bicycles, 7
    ethanol production, 82
    hydroelectricity production, 75
circuit, electrical, 50-51
circular motion, 36
clean energy, 67, 68
clock, effects of motion on, 59
coal, 68
color, 52, 53, 55, 56, 57
combustion chemical reaction, 17, 42
compass, 46, 47
compression, 34, 58
computerized axial tomography, 47
conductivity, 7, 11, 15, 19, 26, 45, 49
conductor, 11, 45, 48, 49, 50
contraction hypothesis, 58
convection, 45
corn, kernel, 83
    See also ethanol
covalent bond, 15
crane, 39, 47, 49, 77
crude oil, 70
    distillation, 71
    global demand for, 71
    reserves, 69, 70, 71
    See also petroleum

D

dam, 69, 74, 75, 88, 89
dark matter, 9
data encryption, 65
data search, 65
DC (direct current), 51
decay chain, (radioactive process) 24, 31
deceleration, 30, 36
decomposition (organic material), 17, 84
degree, 45
Democritus, 6, 8
density, 10, 11, 27
diesel, 71, 82
direct current (DC), 51
distillation, 71, 83
dolphin, biological sonar, 55
dry ice, 9
dry-steam power plant, 86-87
dynamo, 53
dynamometer, 31

E

E=mc² equation, 8, 59
Earth
    atmosphere surrounding, 35
    compass, 46
    friction, 36
    geothermal energy, 68
    gravitational pull, 32, 33, 36
    magnetic field, 46, 47
    movement, measuring, 58
    speed of travel through space, 36
echolocation, 55
ecological cycle, 85
Edison, Thomas Alva, 49, 51
effervescent tablet, solubility, 11
Einstein, Albert, 5, 52
    E=mc² equation, 8, 59
    General Theory of Relativity, 32, 33, 59, 60-61

    gravity, interpretation of, 33, 60
    photoelectric effect, explanation of, 59
    Special Theory of Relativity, 58-59, 60
electric coil, 53
electric current, 15, 50, 51, 56
electric eel, 49
electrical potential, 51
electrical symbol, 51
electricity, 5, 48-49
    applications, 48
    battery, 43, 50
    biogas, 85
    circuits, 50-51
    effects of, 49
    electric current, 48, 50, 51, 56
    electrons in, 48
    hydroelectric energy, 69, 74-75
    hydrogen energy, 90-91
    lightbulb, invention of, 49
    magnetism, applications of, 47
    measuring, units for, 51
    nuclear energy, 76-77
    plasma state, 9
    solar energy, 78-79
    static, 48
    steam engine, 67
    tidal energy, 89
    voltage source, 50
    wind energy, 66-67, 68, 80-81
    worldwide production of, 68
    wireless transmission, 51
electrolysis, 49
electromagnetic field, 52
electromagnetic force, 31
electromagnetic heat loss, 44
electromagnetic radiation, 31
electromagnetic wave
    applications, 53
    discovery of, 52
    redshift, cause of, 61
    travel, speed of, 55
electromagnetism, 47, 49, 52-53
electron, 12, 13, 14, 48, 62
electronics, solar energy use, 79
element, 6, 14-15

    classification of, 4, 14
    periodic table, 14-15
    symbol and number, 14
    types of, 15
endothermal chemical reaction, 17
energy
    chemical, 42
    classification of, 5
    conservation of (law), 38, 42, 45
    daily requirement, adult male, 43
    definition, 4, 42
    electrical, 43
    kinetic, 42
    manifestations of, 28-29, 40
    matter and, 8
    mechanical, 42
    metabolism, 42
    potential, 42, 43
    quantum, 62
    resources, 40-41, 46-47
    sources, 5, 68-69
    transfer of, 43
    transmission of, 63
    worldwide production, 68, 69
    and work, 42-43
    See also specific types, for example solar
        energy
energy efficiency ratio, 43
England: See United Kingdom
enrichment (uranium), 77
ethanol, 82-83
ether, 58
ethylene, 72
exothermal chemical reaction, 17

F

Fahrenheit temperature scale, 45
Faraday, Michael, 52
fermentation (biofuels), 82, 84
Ferris wheel, 36
fertilizing mud, 84, 85

Feynman, Richard, 26
filament (incandescent light), 40-41, 50
fire, 44
fission, 25, 76, 77
FitzGerald, George F., 58, 61
flash-steam power plant, 87
force, 30-31
   centrifugal, 36
   centripetal, 36
   combining and balancing, 30
   contact, 30, 31
   definition of, 30
   fundamental interactions, 31
   measuring, 31
   motion, need for, and, 36
   multiplication of, 5, 38-39
   non-contact, 30, 31
   static, 30
France
   ethanol production, 82
   Rance tidal power plant, 89
Franklin, Benjamin, 48
free electron, 48
free fall, 32
freezing point, 10, 45
frequency, 52, 54
friction, 16, 33, 36, 37, 44
frozen smoke: *See* aerogel
fuel cell, hydrogen-based, 90
fulcrum, 39
fusion, 25, 63

G

Galilei, Galileo, 32
gamma (γ) radiation, 24
gaseous state matter, 9
gasification (natural gas), 73
gasoline, 68, 71, 82, 83
gear system, 38
General Theory of Relativity, 32, 33, 59, 60-61
generator, electrical, 50, 74, 80

geographic pole, 46, 47
geothermal energy, 68, 80, 86-87
Germany
   biodiesel production, 82
   wind farms, 80
gliders (thermal convection), 45
gluon, 13
gold, 12, 19
gravitational lenses, 61
graviton, 31
gravity, 5, 30, 31, 32-33
   black hole, 33
   Einstein's interpretation of, 33, 60
   light rays and, 60
   moon, 10
   roller coaster technology, 33
   weight and, 10
Great Britain: *See* United Kingdom
green energy source, 5, 67
greenhouse effect, 69, 79

H

half-life (radiation), 25
halogen element, 15
hardness, 11, 19
hearing, 54
heat, 44-45
   chemical reactions, 16, 44
   conduction, 45
   convection, 45
   definition of, 44
   electromagnetic losses, 44
   flow, 45
   friction, 44
   measuring, 44
   radiation, 45
   temperature and, 44, 45
   transfer, 45
heat effect (electricity), 49
heat energy, 44
   See also solar energy

Heisenberg, Weiner, 65
helicopter, laws of physics affecting, 37
helium, 21, 44
hertz (Hz), 51, 52
Hertz, Heinrich Rudolf, 52
Hiroshima, atomic bomb, 25
hot-air balloon, 44
Huygens, Christiaan, 57
hydroelectric energy, 69, 74-75
hydrogen, 12, 62
hydrogen energy, 90-91

I-J-K

inclined plane, 38
India, ethanol production, 82
Indonesia, natural gas reserves, 73
industrial fuel, 71
inertia, 36, 37
infrared wave, 52, 57
insulator, 27, 45, 49
interference, 64
invisibility, 27, 57
ionic bond, 15
Iran
   crude oil reserves, 69, 71
   natural gas reserves, 73
Iraq
   crude oil reserves, 71
   natural gas reserves, 73
iron, purification of, 18-19
isotope, 13, 24, 25
Itaipú dam (South America), 75
Italy, biodiesel production, 82
joule, 43
Joule, James P., 45
Jupiter, gravitational strength, 33
Kelvin temperature scale, 45
Kepler, Johannes, 32
kerosene, 71
kinetic energy, 42, 43
Kuwait, crude oil reserves, 71

L

Lagrange, Jacque-Louis de, 36
lanthanide, 14
Lavoisier, Antoine-Laurent, 16
lever, 39
Libya, crude oil reserves, 71
light, 54, 56-57, 58
    black, 57
    color spectrum, 52, 53, 55, 57
    ether, 58
    gravity and, 60
    incandescent, filament, 40-41, 50
    nature of, 52, 56
    reflection, 56
    refraction, 56
    speed of, 55, 56
    visible, wavelength, 6-7, 52
    wave-particle duality, 62
    wave theory of, 57
    white, 57
light effect (electricity), 49
lightbulb, first, 49
lighting, 43, 85
lightning, 43, 48, 49, 55
linear motion, 30, 37
Linné, Carl von, 10
liquefaction (natural gas), 72
liquefied petroleum gas (LPG), 72
liquid state matter, 9
locomotive: See train
Lorentz, Hendrik A., 58, 61
LPG: See liquefied petroleum gas
lubricant, 36, 71

M

machine, simple, 38-39
magnet, 46
magnetic effect (electricity), 49
magnetic field, 46
compass, 46
Earth, 46, 47
electric current, 52
magnetic levitation train (Maglev), 46, 47, 49
magnetic pole, 46, 47
magnetic resonance, 47
magnetism, 5, 30, 31, 46
    applications, 47
Malaysia, natural gas reserves, 73
malleability, 11, 19
Marconi, Guglielmo, 51
Mars, gravitational strength, 33
mass, 10, 42
    conservation of (law), 16
mass number, 14
mathematics
    Newton's contributions to, 3, 32
    theorems, verification of, 65
matter, 8-9
    antimatter, 9
    conservation of (law), 17
    dark, 9
    definition, 8
    elements, 14-15
    energy and, 8
    gaseous state, 9
    liquid state, 9
    properties of, 10-11
    solid state, 8
    structure of, 7
    sublimation, 8-9
    See also atom
Maxwell, James C., 52, 58
Mayer, Julius von, 42, 45
mechanical energy, 42
medicine
    magnetism, applications, 47
    ultrasound, applications, 55
melting point, 10, 11, 14
Mendeleyev, Dimitry, 14
Mercury, orbit, perturbation of, 61
mesoscopic system, 62
metabolism, 42, 45
metal, 18-19, 49
metallic bond, 15
metamaterial, 27
methane gas, 72-73, 85
Michelson, Albert, 58
mirror, 56
Mohs scale, 11
monomer, 20
Moon, gravitational pull, 32, 88
Morley, Edward W., 58
motion, 5, 30, 36-37, 42

N

nanotechnology, 26
nanotube, 4, 26
natural gas, 66, 69, 72-73
    total known reserves, 73
navigation, 46, 47
Neptune, discovery of, 33
neutron, 12, 13, 76
new materials, 26-27
    aerogel, 4, 27
    carbon fiber, 4, 26
    metamaterial, 27
    nanotube, 4, 26
newton, 31
Newton, Isaac, 4, 31, 36
    definition of force, 30
    laws of physics, 28, 37, 58
    light, theory of, 57
    mathematics, contributions to, 3, 32
    motion, theories of, 32, 37
    universal gravity, law of, 30
Nigeria
    crude oil reserves, 71
    natural gas reserves, 73
noble gas, 15, 21
nonmetal element, 15, 21
nonrenewable energy source, 5, 68
    See also specific source, for example
        petroleum
North Pole, 46, 47
Norway, natural gas reserves, 73

nuclear energy, 69, 76-77
nuclear fission: *See* **fission**
nuclear force, 31
nuclear fusion: *See* **fusion**
nuclear weapon, 25
nucleus, atomic, 12, 13, 24, 25, 31

O-P-Q

ocean, tidal energy, 88-89
octet rule, 15
Oersted, Christian, 52
oil: *See* **petroleum**
optical illusion, 56
organic material, 17, 68, 84
oxidation chemical reaction, 17
parabolic motion, 37
particle, 4, 9, 12, 62, 63, 64
particle accelerator, 13
pascal (atmospheric pressure), 34
Pascal, Blaise, 34
periodic table (elements), 14-15
petroleum, 66, 68, 69, 70-71
pH, 23
Philippines, geothermal energy, 87
photoelectric effect, 52, 59
photon, 56
photovoltaic effect, 78
physics, conventional laws of, 5, 28, 37
pig iron, production of, 18-19
Planck, Max, 62, 63
planetary system
  gravitational effects, 32, 33
  orbit, shapes of, 32
plasma state, 9
plastic, 20, 21, 23
polyethelene, annual world production, 21
polymer, 20-21
polymerization, 20
potential energy, 42, 43
power plant
  geothermal, 68, 86-87

nuclear, 76-77
hydroelectric, 74-75
tidal energy, 89
pressure, 11, 34-35
  atmospheric, 35
  bed of nails, fakir's secret, 34, 35
  definition, 34, 35
  gas, 34
  temperature, effect of, 34, 35
  water, 35
propane, 71, 72
proton, 12, 13
pulley, 39
pyrometer, 45
Qatar, natural gas reserves, 73
quanta, 62, 63
quantum computer, 64-65
quantum mechanics, 5, 13, 26, 41, 62-63, 64, 65
quantum numbers, 13
quantum point, 65
quantum superposition, 64
quark, 13
qubit, 64-65

R-S

radar, 53, 55
radiation, 24-25, 45
radio, 52, 53, 54
radioactivity, 24-25
rail transportation: *See* **train**
Rance tidal power plant (France), 89
recycling, 21, 76, 84, 85
redshift, 61
reduction chemical reaction, 17
reflection, 54, 56
refraction, 56
refractive index, 11, 27
relative size, 59
relativity, 5, 41
  General Theory of, 32, 33, 59, 60-61

Special Theory of, 58-59, 60
renewable energy source, 5, 68
  See also specific source, for example **wind energy**
reservoir, 75, 89
resistance, 19, 50, 51
roller coaster, 32-33
Russia
  crude oil reserves, 69, 71
  ethanol production, 82
  natural gas reserves, 73
Rutherford, Ernest, 24
sailboat, 29, 30
satellite communication, 53
satellite navigation, 47
Saudi Arabia
  crude oil reserves, 69, 71
  natural gas reserves, 73
Scanning Tunneling Microscope (STM), 6-7, 63
screw, 38
semiconductor, 15
semimetal element, 15
skin, ultraviolet radiation, 57
slag, 18
soft drink, anhydrous carbon, 83
solar cell, 78-79
solar collector, 79
solar energy, 69, 78-79
solar heating, 79
solar system, magnetic fields, 47
solar water heating, 79
solid state matter, 8, 19
solubility, 11
sonar, 55
sonic boom, 55
sonography, 55
Sorensen, Soren P.L., 23
sound, 5, 54-55
South Pole, 46, 47
space, 5, 33, 58
space technology, solar energy use, 79
Spain, wind farms, 80
Special Theory of Relativity, 58-59, 60
speed
  electromagnetic waves, 55

formula for determining, 37
Mach 1 (sound), 55
SPF: *See* sun protection factor (SPF)
static electricity, 48
static force, 30
steam engine, 34, 68
steel, production of, 19
storage
crude oil, 70
magnetism, applications of, 47
sublimation, 8-9
Sun
gravitational forces, 33
magnetic field, 47
nuclear reactions, 44
SPF, 57
temperature, 44
ultraviolet (UV) radiation, 57
See also **solar cell, solar collector, solar energy, solar radiation, solar system**
sun protection factor (SPF), 57
superconductivity, 9, 51
superfluidity, 9
superheavy element, 15
synthetic rubber, 20

T

telecommunications, 53, 65
teleportation, 65
temperature
absolute zero, 8, 9
heat and, 44, 45
highest recorded, 44
and pressure, effect of, 34, 35
scales, 10, 45
tensile strength, 11
Tesla, Nikola, 51
Thales of Miletus, 47, 48
thermal convection, 45
thermal image, 57
Thomson, Joseph John, 12

Three Gorges Dam (China), 75
tidal energy, 88-89
tidal power plant, 89
timbre, 54
time, 5, 58, 59
train, 34
magnetic levitation (Maglev), 46, 47, 49
transformer, 51, 53
transition metal, 14
transportation
automobile, 43, 79, 90, 91
bicycle, 38-39, 43
magnetism, applications of, 47
solar energy use, 79
train, 34, 46, 47, 49
Trieste (water pressure), 35
tuning fork, 54
tunneling effect, 63
turbine, 34, 28-29
blade, 74, 80, 81
dynamo, 53
hydroelectric energy, 74
jet, newtons generated by, 31
tidal power plant, 88, 89
wind energy, 68, 80-81

U-V

ultrasound, 55
ultraviolet (UV) radiation, 57
uncertainty principle, 13, 62, 65
United Arab Emirates
crude oil reserves, 71
natural gas reserves, 73
United Kingdom, Exeter biogas lighting system, 85
United States
crude oil reserves, 69, 71
ethanol production, 82, 83
geothermal energy, 87
hydroelectric production, 75
natural gas reserves, 73

wind farms, 80
universal gravity, Newton's law of, 30
ununoctium (Uuo 118), 15
uranium, 77
Uranus, gravitational force, 33
UV ray: *See* ultraviolet radiation
vacuum
free fall, 32
motion in, 37
sound, lack of, 54
speed of light in, 58, 59
waves in, 52
valence shell, 14, 15
vaporization, crude oil, 70
Venezuela
crude oil reserves, 71
natural gas reserves, 73
viscosity, 11
volt, 51
voltmeter, 51
volume, 10

W-X-Y

water
chemical composition, 22
geothermal energy, 68, 86-87
hydroelectric energy, 69, 74-75
solar heating, 79
watt, 51
wave, 52, 53, 55
wavelength, 52, 53, 57
weight, gravity, 10
wheel, 39
white light, 57
wind energy, 66-67, 68, 80-81
wireless communication, 52
work, 5, 42-43
xenon, 21
X-ray, 53, 55
Yeager, Charles Elwood, 55
yellowcake, uranium, 77